COFFEE, CODES, & CLICHES

Coffee, Codes, & Cliches

HANNA WALDON

Alex Zandrea Books

To all the hopeless romantics in the world.

And to Romeo; you have a rotten, but beautiful soul. Thank you for believing in me.

Playlist

"Lovin on Me" - Jack Harlow
"Adore You" - Miley Cyrus
"I Met a Girl" - Sam Hunt
"Not to be Dramatic" - Zoe Clark
"Just Pretend" - Bad Omens
"Say You Won't Let Go" - James Arthur
"Mess" - Justin Stone
"Come Back Home" - Sofia Carson
"I Guess I'm in Love" - Clinton Kane
"Chaotic" - Tate McRae
"this is how you fall in love" - Jeremy Zucker, Chelsea Cutler
"Love Me Like You Do" - Ellie Goulding
"Chasing Highs" - Nate Good
"All of Me" - John Legend
"Dive" - Ed Sheeran
"Never Be the Same" - Camila Cabello

Chapter 1

Olivia

It was still dark outside when the automated lights in Olivia's room began to brighten. She groaned and pulled a fluffy pillow over her face, as if that would make a difference. She'd been up into the wee hours of the morning, fighting back against the comma splices and typos that plagued her work life with her dreaded red pen, and being awake felt criminal. She could have slept for another two hours, no question. But then her phone started in with its "gentle wakening" sounds, and it was game over for sleeping. She tossed her pillow to the side, swiped off her alarm, and flopped onto her back, staring at the ceiling. Okay. Time to try and count her blessings. Positives of being awake: plenty of time for a long shower and the ability to make any kind of coffee she wanted. Getting on the metro before rush hour and actually getting to sit down. Making it to work before the office got busy so she could get some things done before everyone started needing things from her. Of course, there was one major negative of being awake after only five hours of sleep: being awake. For a moment, she thought of calling her assistant to say that she would be working from home today—and then remembered that she'd had to fire her assistant, and why she had to fire her assistant, and then she was too grossed out to try to sleep. Well, the world wasn't going to save itself from name changes mid-chapter and people who got into cars twice in the same paragraph. Much less the budget crunch for her business that was starting to make her sweat. "Up and at 'em, kid," she told herself, and rolled out of bed.

She loved her townhouse. She had lived in her crappy apartment for a long time after Small and Sparkling, her web novel publishing company, started to solidify and then actually started making money, making sure that the success was going to last before making any big changes to her personal life. So, feeling comfortable making the purchase, and then remodeling old brick building to be what she wanted it to be...they were all signs of her growing success. Of course, now there was the constantly growing concern that she'd overextended herself after all.

She pushed those thoughts out of her head as best as she could and went to the master bathroom for a shower. She twisted her brown hair up to keep it from getting wet and then stepped into the spray in the glass enclosure, loving that the water was the right temperature and the drain worked correctly. The little luxuries. She washed the sleep out of her eyes and briefly considered using a few other methods to wake herself up...but no. That would not help her with her plan of getting to work a little early.

Her morning routine was simpler than some, more elaborate than others. Toner and a serum before moisturizer, a bit of gel in her hair to make sure it was wavy, not frizzy, and minimal makeup. She'd never gotten the art of much more than a basic eyeliner around her hazel eyes, and she was very bad at lipstick, so she kept everything very basic. Clothing was simple as well. She kept the office at a low-key business casual level, but she'd always been told that the staff would dress one step down from where management was, so she chose gray, tailored slacks and a lightweight sleeveless blouse with a delicate floral pattern for the day. Always flats, though; she was a walking disaster in heels, and she was tall enough that she felt uncomfortable adding more than an inch or so in her day to day anyway. Dressed and prepped for her day physically, it was now time for her favorite part of the morning: coffee.

Coffee had been the fuel of artists and the art-adjacent for centuries, and she had no shame about loving it. It was another way she told herself that she was successful; she didn't have to choose between a cheap drip machine at home or those awful coffee pods at the office job where she answered phones and completed spreadsheets all day long. She'd collected half a dozen different ways to make coffee at home, from simple pour-overs to elegant French presses and a high-end espresso machine. She had a siphon coffee maker that looked like a copper science experiment which she'd dubbed "The Still" in honor of Hawkeye and BJ; last year, her sister Lydia had sent her a Vietnamese phin that she hadn't quite gotten the hang of yet, in part because she never remembered to buy the condensed milk that was key to making the chicory-heavy brew taste heavenly. She chose her morning coffee method like some people trailed their fingers over a collection of expensive watches or designer jewelry. An Americano this morning. Elegant but simple. That would suit her today.

She pushed a series of buttons to start the machine whirring and contemplated the amount of sheer luck that had gone into achieving her biggest dream at the age of 30. *Well, one of my dreams. Still looking for Fitzwilliam.*

Well, even if she hadn't quite found her own romantic hero yet, she'd spent the last five years trying to make sure other people could find theirs—at least, fictional ones. Small and Sparkling was a web novel platform that focused on romance. That in and of itself wasn't unique; every online writing platform that existed was quickly filled with stories that focused on that particular interpersonal aspect of human nature. She'd found, though, that stories on each platform rapidly shifted from a focus on the interplay of personalities that led to emotional intimacy and toward a meditation on the interplay of bodies that led to really great sex. She'd never objected to those stories, and more than one night had found her home alone with a good story and a vibrator, but when she wanted to read something more, well, romantic, she always had to go digging to find the stories marked "sweet" or "intimate" or, even worse, "clean," as if sex were dirty. And the stories she could find rarely had the kind of heat she did want to see, once the couple had fallen for each other—or even while they were falling for each other. She'd been beyond frustrated. So when she found stories that she did want to read, that fit her criteria, she'd started making a list of them. Since they were all online, a webpage with links just made sense. She'd shared it here and there when other people expressed similar interests. And then it broke containment, and suddenly she was getting thousands of visitors who were not only following her links, but suggesting other stories that could be listed along with recommending their own. It made sense to let people share their stories, and the webpage creation plan she'd bought had plenty of storage space. So she'd started letting people publish their own stories, chapter by chapter, on her site. News of that spread, and then suddenly she was being approached not for her list, but for the opportunity to publish on her site.

Presented with that opportunity, she found that she wanted these stories to have a real website to show them off, not just some cut and paste free template on a generic page. She knew just enough about web design to get herself in trouble, so she'd kept things going so far, but as interest had shifted, she'd decided to shoot her shot and see if she could make something that would be far more than just a list—instead, it would be a destination. She'd used the inheritance she'd gotten from her grandparents to get started while she crowdfunded a campaign to build a platform where people could read the same kind of stories she liked. She'd done everything she could to make it inclusive, inviting in stories from every kind of couple (or thruple, or polycule) that was presented to her, as long as they were focused on love and finding it. It was all niche, but the people who wanted that niche really wanted it. She felt like she was making a difference to people, even if it was just in her little corner of the world, and how many 30-year-olds could say that?

She'd find her own romance eventually. Probably. If so many people wrote about it, it had to be out there somewhere.

While her coffee brewed, she made herself some scrambled eggs, then sat down to the second most important part of her morning ritual. She had a small, four-person table in her kitchen, and next to the salt and pepper shakers and the little napkin holder was a worn paperback copy of Jane Austen's *Pride and Prejudice*, i.e., one of the most important romance novels of all time. This was the third copy she'd owned in her life. One she'd gotten in her teens and had worn out before high school graduation; the second had given up the ghost just after college. She'd had a digital copy for a while after that, but while the entire rest of her life seemed to occur on a tablet or a computer screen, this was the one of the few things that she liked best on paper.

This copy was starting to show its age. She'd already had to reinforce the spine with library tape, but the glue in the binding itself was getting loose. Some pages in the middle were starting to wiggle. But it did well for a glue-bound, mass market paperback that she practically used as a morning devotional. She'd used those little moveable sticky flags, the ones that didn't damage the paper, to mark her favorite scenes, and then color coded them: Lizzy being snarky, Darcy being awkward, funny moments with Mr. Collins. Sometimes she started the book from the beginning and read through it, a regular bookmark chasing her favorite characters through their pages. Sometimes she just flipped open to what she wanted to read. This morning, she thought of Darcy's first confession, the one that was constantly quoted, which was so funny because it was one of his most entertaining failures in the entire book. But he ended up pulling it together in the end. He won the girl through his actions, and the book ended happily ever after.

"In vain I have struggled. It will not do," she said, quietly, flipping to the appropriate page. "My feelings will not be repressed. You must allow me to tell you how ardently I admire and love you." Elizabeth's indignant response would fortify her for what was sure to be a long day. But she hadn't even gotten to Lizzy's furious reply when her phone buzzed loudly, demanding her attention.

She almost sent the unknown caller to voicemail, but decided to pick up the phone at the last minute. She barely got out a greeting, and then she just listened to the caller—one of her authors, as it happened—scream in frustration and rage. She let Jenny McLarson yell herself out, feeling her own tension ratchet up one, two, three, four notches. "So let me get this straight," Olivia said, when there was a break in the very well deserved rant. "The update pushed live with a typo, and now, instead of it turning out that Jessica and Devon are on the verge of reconciling and saving their marriage, it seems that Jessica has been sleeping with Devon's twin brother, Tyler. I see." She wanted to scream, but it wouldn't help anything. "Of course. I'm going to hang up with you and get this all fixed immediately. I'll call you when I'm at the office. I'm so sorry about this. You have my word that it will be handled in the next hour. And I'm so sorry."

The call disconnected, and Olivia let her head fall back against the wall with a bit of a thwack. "I really need to hire an assistant," she told the air. The air, shockingly, did not respond.

Chapter 2

Thomas

Thomas stared at himself in the full-length mirror for another minute, adjusting his tie for the third time. He sighed. It was impossible for him to feel more out of place than he did right now. He was standing in his best friend's luxurious, top-floor penthouse in the center of one of the more important cities in the country in an off-the-rack shirt and slacks, adjusting a tie that had probably cost more than his plane ticket. "You're sure I need a tie?" It wasn't a question really. Mason had already said 'yes' three times.

"Yes!" Four times.

He sighed and straightened the tie again. Everything else about him looked reasonable. Mason had attacked him with some kind of hair wax to get his sandy blond hair to lay smoothly instead of falling in his eyes, and the suit fit him as well as something was going to when it wasn't tailored. He wasn't an easy guy to fit, sometimes.

He was tall and broad shouldered, but thick through the chest and waist. Suits tended to be too tight in one area or the other. But this tie? This tie was a nightmare. There was a joke at home. What did you call the man in the three-piece suit? The deceased. Cue laughter. At least Mason hadn't tried to go that far.

Everything about today felt off. It wasn't that he thought he'd come to the big city and some tech company would snatch him up off the street, screaming that whatever genius idea was in his brain at that exact moment was going to be the next big disrupter, or at least get a few hundred people playing something on their cell phones while they were in the bathroom. But he hadn't anticipated two months of not even getting an acknowledgement of his application. This job was much, much better than nothing, but personal assistant at a publishing house was definitely not what he'd had in mind for himself at graduation. Along with only getting the job due to his best friend's connections.

Mason's friend Callie had assured him that he'd be perfect for the job, and a hundred times better than the last assistant. He could type more than 60 words per minute, for one thing, and he also knew that Microsoft Word had a "track changes" feature. Thomas had been around computer science students for too long; he'd forgotten that those were things people had to be told.

"Are you done yet?"

Thomas sighed. This damn tie was probably as good as it was going to get. "Yeah."

In the kitchen, Mason, his best friend and the owner of the condo, had left out the bagels. Thomas popped one into the toaster and then stuck one of those weird little pod things into the machine to get a cup of coffee. He wasn't finicky about coffee, in general, but he didn't love tossing the little plastic cups away every day. If he'd gone out and bought a regular coffee pot, Mason would have made room for it on the gleaming kitchen counters without a moment of complaint. Mason had been crystal clear: his invitation for Thomas to come and stay in the condo while he got his feet under himself had no strings and no obligations, no time limits, and no cost. When Mason's father had died suddenly when they were in college, Thomas had been there for him; according to Mason, that made them better than brothers, and whatever he could do to help, he would.

That had included, it turned out, pulling strings to find Thomas a job when it became clear that it was going to take some time to find one on his own. Mason seemed much less surprised about this than Thomas was. It was just how Mason's world of high-powered investors and business worked, apparently. You got work through connections and contacts, not through applications and begging. Once Mason had offered him help, Thomas had vaguely considered that Mason might find him some kind of a job at a tech company. Assistant to a woman who published romance novels was not the starting point he anticipated. Mason insisted that Thomas would be doing a favor for him, and he could certainly keep looking for other things at the same time. Since Mason was footing the bill for absolutely everything in the apartment, Thomas was making his savings last, but he'd have to start paying on his student loans next month. He could even start saving for his own apartment. Probably not in the city itself, the cost of rent made his eyebrows hit his hairline when he started looking around, but somewhere within driving distance. Or, hell, most jobs in his field were remote these days anyway.

The point was, therefore, that he wasn't going to waste this opportunity, even if it didn't look anything like what he wanted for his life over time.

The bagel popped up, and Mason slid the cream cheese across the counter for him. With his bagel correctly smeared and his coffee in hand, he sat down at the kitchen bar next to Mason—who had made himself some kind of poached egg with a sauce and fried ham. And possibly home fries. That man did love to cook.

"So, when you get there," Mason said, "Ask for Callie. She's got everything lined up."

"And I don't have to interview?"

"Nope. I'm sure she'll have to introduce you around and whatever else, but she says it's fine. Something weird happened with the last assistant. She won't tell me about it, just shudders when I ask." He laughed. "If you can get the story out of anyone, do it, it'll be nice to have something to bug her with later."

Mason and Callie had been friends since preschool, according to Mason. Thomas had met her once while they were in school. She'd seemed like a nice girl, short and peppy, and when the three of them went out, she'd bought drinks when it was her turn. He'd heard a million stories about her, but that was his only first-hand experience. Thomas nodded in ascent to his fact-finding mission.

"And you did your research?" Mason asked.

"What?"

"You know what you're going into?"

"A... job as an assistant to a publisher?"

Mason did not roll his eyes, but it looked like it took an effort of will. "A romance publisher. Of online web novels. That is differentiated from the competition by its focus on romance instead of erotica. Although they don't hold back on the sexy parts, when it seems right for the story. Have you even looked at their webpage?" At Thomas's blank expression, Mason grabbed his phone, tapped at it for a minute, then shoved it over at him. "They're called Small and Sparkling, which is a reference to both the serial nature of their stories—most updates are less than 5000 words—and engagement rings. Read their 'About' page. Note the Jane Austen quote at the end. You'll be able to use that; according to Callie, that's basically the company's thesis statement."

Thomas read over the description of the company's mission and goals. It was targeted, focused, just long enough to compel the customer but not long enough to bore them. Impressive. He'd managed to get his English minor mostly in composition classes while focusing his literature interests more on the history of science fiction. He'd never read Jane Austen or any of the 19th century society novels, and he didn't recognize the quotation Mason had pointed out at all, "The first moment I beheld him, my heart was irrevocably gone." He tried to memorize it.

"Olivia Michaelson, the owner," Mason continued, "is also the shit, she knows her stuff. She crowdfunded the site, which anyone can do with promises, but she made it actually happen, which is a lot harder." He started ticking points off on his fingers. "She focuses on the parts she has to handle; she delegates like a boss—literally—she networks in the business community, and she does it all backwards in heels."

Thomas nodded at the Ginger Rogers reference, always one of his favorites.

"I'm not saying she's going to help you make your name as a programmer, but there are much worse allies to have when you start looking at running your own company someday."

"I've never said that's my goal."

Mason waved him off. "The only way to make the kind of changes you want to make is to do them on your own. But that's at least five years into your ten-year plan."

"I have a ten-year plan?"

"Well, technically, I have a ten-year plan for us. In five years, you're going to have a business idea that I'm so excited by that I'm going to invest in it, and then we're going to take over the world."

"And thus spoke the business major. Thanks for clue-ing me in."

"Happy to do it." Mason looked him up and down and sighed. "Who taught you to tie a tie, your kindergarten teacher?"

Chapter 3

Olivia

She didn't even bother trying to leave the house until she'd called editorial to have them pull down the chapter, fix the absolutely ridiculous error, and repost the chapter. She called PR to have them push something to the main page with an apology for their error and customer service to have them refund tokens for those readers who had bought the chapter with the major, absurd error that violated one of the utterly inviolable rules of romance writing: the heroine never cheats.

Once that fire was out, she had editorial go over the rest of the updates pushed this morning to look for any other major issues that might have been missed somehow. She called Jenny back and groveled. Promised a bonus for the inconvenience. And Jenny wasn't unreasonable; thankfully, her readers were so loyal to her that they'd immediately started blaming Small and Sparkling rather than the author herself. And since it was their fault, that was fair, if frustrating.

The next step was to get into the office and figure out how the fuck this had happened in the first place. She packed her second cup of coffee in a travel mug, all day-dreaming about beating rush hour absolutely gone, and headed out the door. Depressingly, at this point, taking the metro to work would be faster than driving.

The Small and Sparkling offices were in a modest building in one of the outer neighborhoods of the city; when she took the metro, she was normally able to get another twenty minutes of work done. She'd done less direct editing over the past few years and begun spending more of her time on the behind the scenes work that kept the servers whirring and the lights on. For a little while, when everyone was stuck at home without a lot to do, readership had ballooned, and she'd been forced to hire extra staff in all departments to keep things afloat. But the boom across the tech industry had died out as many people had gone back to work and had less free time again. She'd managed to cut a few corners by letting most of her workforce stay remote and hoping that readership would climb again as people settled back into their new normal, but the numbers hadn't been adding up for a few months now. She'd dipped into her savings a few times to plug the holes in the dam, but that wasn't a sustainable solution. She had yet another meeting with financial this week to stare at numbers and try to figure out a solution that didn't involve laying off a quarter of her staff. There had to be something.

As she got off the metro and headed up the escalator to the street, her phone started to ding with a series of incomprehensible notifications. First, there was a series of updates from her calendar as the same meeting was scheduled and removed, then rescheduled, then moved back to the original time. Next, it was half a text followed by two emojis, then a message on the company's internal message board that was something about 'Eva extension last upside down call'? She put her phone back in her purse, determined to ignore it until she was in the building. If she was getting sensible messages from a real assistant, responding to them on the go would make sense. Trying to figure out what the in the name of all that was holy Callie was messaging her about while also not walking into cars was not going to happen. She'd be in the building in five minutes, and Callie could explain what was happening then.

Having her director of marketing and outreach, who was also her best friend, serve as her assistant had been a terrible idea, but at the time, it had been the least terrible option. Hell, she hadn't even had an assistant for the first three years Small and Sparkling had been around; other departments had always needed the budget more than she n3eeded someone to keep track of her own calendar. But when everyone was suddenly stuck at home and a major trade journal had mentioned her site as a great way to get a little bit of hope into the day, suddenly everyone who had time to read a chapter of a story every day was knocking on her digital door. Everything had happened all at once. The site needed to be able to handle more people—a lot more people—and she'd needed more people screening potential writers, more editors, more customer service. Everything had expanded so fast that she hadn't been able to keep track of anything, and having an assistant, someone who could screen the world for her so that she could focus was the most critical thing in the world. It let her get her job done.

She'd originally pulled a guy, Jackson, off the customer service team who seemed to know his way around a scheduling calendar and workflow software. He'd done an incredible job for the next three years; she got quick, concise messages, email lists, neatly prioritized to-do items, and run-downs on everyone she was about to meet so that she could walk into a room with a smile and a can-do attitude. He was also helpful because Small and Sparkling was not the only short fiction website he liked, so he'd been able to give her invaluable insight into what some of the other story platforms were doing, helping her differentiate Small and Sparkling from the competition.

The only problem with Jackson was that it turned out he'd enjoyed some of the stories a just a little too much. In an office supply closet. Someone from IT went looking for some paperclips and had found him at the penultimate moment of his enjoyment, leading to an incredibly messy situation. Olivia had needed to pay for dry cleaning and two weeks of leave for the IT employee. She'd scrubbed the shelves herself. Jackson had been informed that, if he tried to enter the building again, a restraining order would be followed. For his part, he was humiliated that he'd been caught white-handed, as it were, and promised that he would never darken the company's doorstep again.

That had been a month ago. Olivia had thought she could go without an assistant, figuring she could save the company at least one person's salary, but a week had shown her how impossible that was. Her job had gotten bigger along with the company, and she couldn't keep track of all the things that she needed to do, who she needed to meet with, or what department head had an urgent request that couldn't be put off. She'd pulled in Callie for help until she could figure out the next step. After three weeks, she wasn't sure if Callie was completely incompetent for the role or dead set determined to make it look like she was so that Olivia would hire someone else, and Callie could go back to her (incredibly important) job of managing the limited and customized print subscriptions and overall marketing efforts. She suspected it was a mix of the two.

As she walked into the building and toward the elevator, she sent Callie a message: *I'm on the way up*. When the elevator doors dinged open again, Callie was standing outside them with a tablet in her hand. Olivia waved her phone in Callie's face. "What does this even mean? Eva extension what?" She made sure that her tone was funny, not mean, and got a smile from Callie in return. Which was good, because the entire situation was so frustrating that Olivia was rapidly losing patience with it.

"Sorry," Callie said. Callie was small and incredibly blonde, perky, and cheerful. She fell into pace with Olivia as Olivia walked toward her office and didn't seem to experience a hint of shame over her incomprehensible message. "Allison Vee. She's the writer on *A Chance to Breathe*?"

"Right." *A Chance to Breathe* was one of the first series Olivia had published. It was an incredible ongoing story, updated three times a week, and had the sweeping scope of the very best primetime soap operas. It had started out as a second-chance friends-to-lovers—two best friends from childhood who had grown apart, lived their separate lives, and then come back together to fall in love—and had grown from there. The original couple was long since married with children, but Allison's story had been happily spinning through an entire cast of characters that she'd slowly introduced over time, transferring the novel from one couple to the next with a seamlessness that had left Olivia stunned. It was one of the best things she'd ever published, and somehow, the audience kept growing regardless of the pairing Allison was focusing on at the time.

"She says that her schedule is upside down, and she needs an extension. No, wait." Callie studied her notes more carefully. Olivia glanced over at Callie's scribbles.

Callie put incredible effort into choosing just the right font for each month's print subscription gift box, but she wrote like a physician. Of course, that could be why she'd gotten good at fonts. "Eva's story is upside down and therefore she needs an extension so she can schedule revisions." She squinted at her screen some more.

"I'll just call her," Olivia said. They'd reached her office, and Callie pulled the door open for her like she was a character in a movie about a much fancier businesswoman than she was. "What else?"

Callie swiped around on her tablet and Olivia tried not to stamp her foot. It would be petty as well as unhelpful, and she was only willing to do one of those at a time. "A couple other messages. I'll email them to you. I put a couple of meetings on your calendar, I'll get you some notes about them. Oh, and your new assistant is in the conference room."

Olivia was torn between relief at the idea of dealing with someone—anyone—who was better at this than Callie and being more than a little frustrated at the phrasing. "Sorry, my what?"

Callie gave her wide, innocent eyes, and Olivia tried not to scoff. Callie had been one of the first people Olivia brought on to help with the crowdfunding campaign; she had literally been part of Small and Sparkling since the beginning. "Remember, I told you that I was going to find you a new assistant, since I'm so shockingly bad at it and my talents are so wildly needed elsewhere?"

"I remember agreeing to putting out a job posting and reaching out to temp agencies. I definitely don't remember seeing resumes from candidates, scheduling interviews, making a decision, and then hiring someone. Callie, what the hell?" Olivia dropped her bag on the floor and started sorting through the mess of stuff that had accumulated on her desk overnight. When she was one of the last people to leave and one of the first people into the office, how the hell did so much stuff end up on her desk? If only Jackson had been kind enough to jerk off in the bathroom.

Callie gave an overly dramatic sigh. "Look, I've only met Thomas a few times, but one of my oldest friends vouches for him. He needs a job, and you need an assistant, and I really need you to have an assistant. He knows how to use Office and he can type without looking at his keyboard. Mason said he's a programmer, so he'll be able to figure out our project software and pipeline easily. I just need you to sign off."

"Fair, and I'd be happy to have him meet with HR to see if he's a qualified candidate before moving through the rest of the hiring process." Jesus, she could practically feel the stick sliding up her ass as she said it.

"Sure, sure," Callie said. "And that's what I originally told Mason, that I'd try and make sure that Thomas at least got to meet with you for an interview. The problem is that there seems to have been some miscommunication somewhere, and Thomas turned up here with his driver's license and social security card ready to go. He absolutely thinks it's his first day."

"Ah." The picture was getting clearer. "And you didn't have the heart to tell him there was a misunderstanding?"

"I...no. No, I did not." Callie smiled conspiratorially. "I also think it should be noted that he is really gorgeous. Not just cute, like, handsome. Very."

Olivia raised an eyebrow as she sat down, pulling things out of her bag to add to the many stacks of... stuff. "After what we just went through, you want me to hire someone strictly based on their attractiveness?"

Callie shrugged, still grinning. "Jackson was totally normal looking, and look what happened there? This guy is adorable, he's probably swimming in whatever kind of partners he wants. Way less of a sexual harassment risk."

"Just have to keep you from harassing him first, apparently." She looked at Callie for a long minute, then rolled her eyes. "Fine, fine. I'll meet with him at least. I'm making absolutely no promises. He has to be able to at least type. But since that's an upgrade from my current assistant..."

If they hadn't been in the office, Callie might have tossed a pillow at her; Olivia would have thrown it right back. Since they were being professional, Callie gave her a work-appropriate nod. "Okay, boss. I'll let him know you'll be in in...what, ten minutes?"

"Give me fifteen. I need to call Allison." *And figure out what she was actually trying to tell me.*

"You got it."

"Shut the door, okay?"

Callie shut the door as she walked out.

Oliva spun her chair slowly in a circle, taking in the office, the view, her company in general. She'd insisted on a small office, joked that she didn't need a huge amount of square footage to tell herself that she was important to the business, but really, she'd just wanted this view. They were on the seventh floor of their building, and she had a gorgeous view out over the city. She had one row of bookcases in the office, and she'd filled them with books, but she'd skipped the typical all-matched leatherbound set. She'd filled one case with dictionaries, writing manuals, guides to character and plot creation. And then she'd slowly started filling up the rest of the shelves with romance novels. Old classics, like Danielle Steele and Nora Roberts and Beverly Jenkins, paired with modern geniuses like Courtney Milan and Alisha Rai and Jennie Lin, and queen of them all, the almighty Jane Austen.

"Jane," she said, trying to speak back through time. "We gotta get this fixed. Somehow. You and me. Alright?"

Chapter 4

Thomas

Thomas sat alone in a fancy conference room in a borrowed tie and tried to maintain his calm. He'd gone where Mason told him to go and asked for Callie like he'd been told to. But when he said that he was there for his first day, Callie got a look of complete panic in her eyes for a moment before sticking him in here. He had a sinking feeling that some wires had gotten crossed, there was no job, and Callie had gone off to find someone else to tell him that so that she didn't have to piss off one of her oldest and best friends. He'd been sitting on his thumbs for about thirty minutes and was seriously considering just getting up and leaving. If there wasn't anything here for him, then he should be out there, looking for something else. Yeah, programming jobs were a little thin on the ground given that every tech company had been laying off people left and right as all the services that had been absolutely desperate when everyone was trapped at home became a lot less urgent when they were back to their daily commutes. His dad had always insisted that applications were a numbers game. You just had to send out so many that a 'yes' was basically a mathematical certainty. His father, a math professor at a major midwestern university, was perfectly aware that that wasn't how statistics worked. But even his father could sometimes let the facts slide in order to be encouraging to his son, even though Thomas had eschewed what his father saw as the inherent beauty of "pure math." It was, after all, a display of his father's regard that no one had objected to his English minor in school.

As much as he'd always loved tearing into novels and figuring out what made them tick, however, it didn't pay the bills. And he loved programming. Something about using code to paint a useable and interactive picture that achieved a tangible goal just blew his mind. And it might let him get a job that would actually let him get a mortgage and eventually help support a family instead of funneling him into a career as an academic or a waiter. Mason was doing him a tremendous favor by letting him stay at his condo while he looked for someone who agreed that "there should be an app for that," but he would prefer not to live his life being chased by creditors. He could wait until Olivia Michaelson got here, no matter how long it took.

Before his mind could take too desperate of a turn down that direction, however, the conference room door opened, and the most beautiful woman he could remember seeing walked in. She was tall, with long brown hair swept up in that kind of messy bun that seemed to take just as long to arrange as the fancy, slicked-back version. He guessed that she was in her late 20s or early 30s. Logical assumption was that she was the head of Small and Sparkling, also known as the person who held his current fate in the palm of her nicely manicured hand.

He stood up as she entered the room and managed to stumble through some basic pleasantries without completely scrambling his words, which was a relief. She gave him a pleasant, professional smile, and something about it just wiped him out entirely. It made him think of taking away all those layers of professionalism and seeing what was there underneath. In a level of graphic detail that was almost embarrassing, he was sure he knew what her hair would feel like between his fingers and the shape her pretty mouth would make when he leaned down to kiss her.

Thomas shook his head to clear his thoughts. Product of stress and nerves, clearly; between fighting with his clothing and enduring another ten minutes of Mason's alternating coaching and quizzing about Small and Sparkling and Olivia Michaelson specifically, he had already been on edge this morning without a hint of a break. And he'd noticed how pretty Olivia was when he was looking her up on various platforms on his way into the office. It was her poise now that left him fascinated with her. There was something very elegant about how she sat, how she folded her hands in front of herself, and how she smiled at him.

"So, Thomas. I'm Olivia," she said. "As I'm sure you heard, I'm looking for a new assistant. Thanks for coming in." She set down a bound green notebook in front of her and opened to a fresh page. She turned a smile on him that would have made his heart go bounce around in his chest if he let it do such absurdly unprofessional things.

Thomas wasn't entirely sure what to make of any of it. Thanks for coming in, have a nice day, don't darken the doorstep again? Or thanks for coming in, here's a pile of paperwork to fill out for HR and be ready to get to work this afternoon? He went with a basic and easy, "Thanks for seeing me." New plan. There was no way they'd send the head of the company into the room just to tell him that he should just leave, so, worst case scenario, he was starting an interview. So. Interview face, interview smile, interview listening to every syllable and wondering why it felt like a voice he could hear forever, and he forced himself to push through that to hear her actual words.

"I'm sorry, we've been a little disorganized this last week, and I didn't get a copy of your resume before we met today. Would you mind walking me through a little bit of your work history?" What a polite way to say that she didn't have it, because he'd never even given it to Mason. She made it sound so calm and cool, not at all like there was some kind of massive screwup underway.

"Well, my degree is in computer science, so a lot of my work has been internships or volunteer work at businesses that are looking for programming, engineering, and similar skills. I did minor in English and worked in my school's writing lab as a tutor for two years, though." They sounded like weak mentions to him, but his rapid texting with Mason had convinced him that every skill he could link to the company or the position would be helpful.

Olivia was nodding. "So if your skills and education are focused in that direction, why a publishing company? And why this position?"

He thought about spinning some bullshit at her about how he was secretly passionate about the book industry and what he wanted more than anything was to follow in her footsteps and create a micro fiction platform for science fiction and psychological horror (which he would absolutely check out if someone else did it, but was completely uninterested in building himself). But there was something about this put-together woman that pushed him into a pretty no-bullshit explanation. "It's the job that's available. There are more transferable skills between these two positions than you think. I'm good with computers, clearly, I know my way around a project layout and team management software, and I know that deadlines cannot be violated for any reason short of act of God or natural disaster if you want to avoid crunch. And avoiding crunch is always the goal."

Olivia nodded along. "Tell me something about that English minor."

Of course she was interested in that. "It was pretty general, all things considered. It may be stereotypical, but I loved the most was science fiction, especially the foundations of the genre. The idea of Victor Franken-stein, this guy playing with forces we did not understand, maybe were not supposed to understand, with absolute confidence and not a lot of ethical understanding...it was fascinating." Olivia was nodding along, so he risked an addition. "One of the thing that science, computer or otherwise, doesn't always spend enough time thinking about is ethical ramifications. Like that quote from the movie, about how we were so excited that we could do it that we didn't think about if we should. So much of science fiction is like 'don't build AI, it'll destroy our civ-ilization and then kill us', and then some tech bro goes and invents a program to write books and draw art for us, like that's any kind of a good idea." There was a whole digression there about how some of the most popular 'AI' programs people talked about hadn't been allowed to learn anything new since 2019, so were barely out-of-date word prediction programs, but he didn't figure that a deep dive into the intricacies of neural nets was necessary or helpful at this point. Still, she didn't have that bored, disengaged look that people sometimes got when he talked about more than how to install a good adblocker on their web browser. He reminded himself of what Mason had said: Olivia had built the earliest versions of Small and Sparkling as her own reference tool. She at least knew her way around a free webpage builder, and that was more than a lot of people could handle.

She held her journal the way some people held their cell phones, comfortable and easy. Quick notes (something for him to worry about), long notes (something to worry about), nothing (something to worry about), but she kept writing. He could only take that as a good sign; it was clear at a glance that this book was an important tool for her. When she'd set it down on the table, he'd noted what looked like a start date of three months ago on the front cover, but she'd made her way through a quarter of the journal already based on the tabs sticking out from the pages. As she leaned over and he tried desperately to only stare in ways that were work appropriate, he could see grids, lists, and thick paper that was slightly waved and bent from use instead of just a journal that was pretty for the sake or being pretty. The remainder of the book was utterly pristine, untouched. So much work done already, with so much left to do. Thomas took a breath, trying to shake off the thought of what about her was untouched and could be filled.

His sister Abby was obsessed with a journalling method that she harassed him about, insisting some part of his life should be analog. Bullet journaling? Was that was she called it? He'd call and ask and figure it out if Olivia would just let him work.

Olivia gave him an up-and-down look that was more shrewd than he would have expected. His heart started to beat too fast, suddenly convinced that she was going to tell him she wanted someone more touchy feely, more...well, feminine for the role.

"I'm sorry, I have to ask some blunt questions here," she said.

He nodded.

"Do you read romance, at all?"

Lying would be stupid. She'd ask follow up questions. "I haven't previously, no." Insisting that he was willing to learn the product was ridiculous; he'd always been told that doing so implied that the interviewee was desperate. He was, but there was no need to advertise that.

He had looked over the website when he was on the train over, and had been surprised at the breadth of genres that fit into the romance category on her site. He always thought of romance stories as soap operas set in hospitals or a woman in a corset having her delicate inner flower pierced by his mighty sword. Instead, he'd found spy novels, gender-bending spaceship captains, a pirate princess taking on a fantasy world, steam punk— every genre he'd ever appreciated. They just all had the common theme of also talking about people who were falling in love with other people. It had made him want to dig in a little bit, understand it all a little bit better. Part of that was his programming brain; he loved taking things apart and understanding them so that he could create them in new forms. But trying to insist he'd investigate more about the product when he was just trying to get a job would be weird; he just tried to make sure that his tone seemed interested, light, and not even remotely dismissive. "I do think that what you're doing on the website is pretty exciting. It's like you're bringing back serial stories from the 19th century. Like Charles Dickens and his crew." Crew? Had he seriously just said crew?

That got earned him another one of those pretty smiles. It had been a long time since he'd swooned over a woman's smile, and he needed to not be thinking this way about his potential boss.

"I appreciate that," she said. "I have encountered some resistance from people, over the years, who refuse to take romance seriously. Who argue that because our stories talk about love, they're somehow less important than other types of fiction."

He didn't have to fake indignance. His mother had lived for her subscription to Harlequin Desire. "That's ridiculous," he said. "I mean, I know romance isn't for everybody, and all respect in the world to aromantic people, but there's nothing wrong with wanting to read about some people falling in love. Dumping on people for their happiness is casual cruelty, not an opinion."

She was leaning forward now, a light flush in her cheeks, and he knew he'd broken through that professional exterior, at least a little. It sparked something hot in him, and he had to consciously distract himself to make sure that he wasn't reacting in a way that wouldn't be useful in an interview. If he met her alone, somewhere dark and steamy, with throbbing music and no consequences?

No. Absolutely not. Stop that.

"Do you know the cardinal rule of romance stories?"

She sounded conspiratorial, like she was imparting a trade secret that he could use as a hack for the entire concept of romance. "I'm sorry, I don't."

She grinned, and heat shot through him. "Happy endings."

"What?"

"Happy endings," she repeated. She leaned back in her chair like she had just explained the Arc of the Covenant. The neckline of her sleeveless top had slipped to the side a bit, and he could see the edge of a pale blue broad strap and freckles on her neck. He was going to need to sit for a minute before walking out of this room if he wasn't going to be completely and utterly embarrassing.

"That's it?"

She nodded. "The couple ends up happy together. There's a sense that they'll be together, at least for the foreseeable future. That's all. Every few years, someone comes along and is all 'oh, I'll deconstruct the genre and at the end they won't be happy,' like that's not every other book in the known universe. We make a safe space for happy endings. That's it. That's the whole secret of romance. Our readers show up trusting that, when the story ends, they can believe in romantic love for a little bit. Hopefully, they can believe in it for themselves. That's the whole thing."

"'I have been meditating on the very great pleasure which a pair of fine eyes in the face of a pretty woman can bestow,'" he said, the words rolling around in his mouth like a whiskey he hadn't appreciated right away, but the underlying warmth had finally struck home.

It seemed like Olivia had spent most of the interview smiling at him, and he wanted very much to keep that smile happening. No doubt about it. He was completely smitten with her, and if she didn't want to hire him, he'd be trying to figure out to take her out on a date. "Fitzwilliam Darcy, *Pride and Prejudice*, nice. Fine, you're hired. At least for the week. And then we'll see how it's going."

Even the happiness caused by hearing that didn't stop him from wondering what a date would be like with his new boss.

Chapter 5

Olivia

Olivia had absolutely not intended to hire this wet-behind-the-ears computer science major who obviously knew nothing about anything her company was doing. Callie had certainly been right that he was nice to look at, though. He looked tall and broad through the shoulders, but he had a barrel chest that made his suit not quite fit right. He had sandy blond hair that looked like it had a nice wave, and if it hadn't been waxed into place, she was pretty sure it would fall directly in his eyes. It would make him look ridiculously young, younger than the early twenties she assumed he would be. His face was more strong than handsome; straight nose, broad cheekbones, deep-set eyes, and a clear jawline, but there was nothing that would make her kick him out of bed for eating cookies. When he smiled, his entire body lit up, and that voice. Jesus. He had a soft, charming tone that slid directly from her ears into her panties and made her think very inappropriate thoughts. But it was the Darcy quote that flipped some switch for her. He was passionate about something, and even if it was just getting the job, that would be a reason to focus on his work. At the risk of being mercenary, she knew damn well how thin on the ground IT jobs were; the economy in general was just one of the many reasons she wanted to avoid laying off people as long as possible. Even if he did want to jump ship for a job with a tech company, it was probably going to take a little while for him to find something, and maybe he'd be able to fix the mess her calendar and to-do list had become in the last month before taking off. Jackson had had a system in place, but it had been a system unique to his brain, and given the rapid nature of his departure, he hadn't really been in a place to share his knowledge with a colleague to create a smooth transition.

The Darcy line was something that Thomas could have Googled in the conference room while waiting for her, but even that said something about his willingness to engage with what Small and Sparkling was doing. Finding people who didn't look down on romance stories had been a challenge she had faced since she was a teenager; the good news had always been that romance readers were the most passionate and engaged readers that existed, at least in the US. And the fact that he was willing to care about it at least that much? That was pretty great, all things considered.

The nice to look at factor hadn't hurt her feelings at all, either. And he didn't seem to be too displeased by her appearance, either. He had been reasonably subtle about it, but she'd noticed his gaze sliding up and down her as soon as she'd entered the conference room. She'd let herself be flattered by it. She generally tried to avoid the societal push that women over the age of 29 were basically expired and going to be sad, lonely, cat-owning spinsters for the rest of their lives, but the attention of a guy who had probably graduated from college in the last six months stroked her ego.

"One last question," she asked. "How good are you at making coffee?"

It was the first time she'd seen him stumble since the completely-not-an-interview had started. "I'm...fine, I guess? I'm not good at latte art that can be shared on social media, but I can push a button?"

She pouted just a little before she got herself under control. The way his eyes darted to her lower lip made her breath catch just a little. Oh, she was going to need to be so careful. With an estimated age difference of 8 or 9 years, he was already forbidden fruit to her, but add in the fact that she was going to be his direct superior, and she was going to need to keep him six feet away at all times. And if he was going to keep looking at her like that, she was going to need bras thick enough to hide her tightening nipples. And maybe buy a better vibrator. There was playing with fire and there was staring into a volcano.

Olivia hadn't been in a relationship for more than a year, and the people she'd dated before that were...less than inspirational, in a romantic sense. None of them had been bad people, or even specifically bad for her, just underwhelming. She considered herself a romantic, but it wasn't like she expected flowers at work every day and rose petals in the bathtub every night. She just wanted something more than physical companionship. She wanted someone to send her pictures of a cloud shaped like something silly that had made them think of her, or to text a snippet of poetry that had brought her to mind. Something to know that they were thinking of her when she wasn't standing directly in front of them. It didn't seem like all that much to ask.

When she was being generous, she could admit that she was so busy that making any of that happen was hard on her end, too. But to have none of it directed toward her made it harder for her to be vulnerable enough to ask for it. As a teenager, she never would have dreamed that a link to a song with "this made me think of you" would be such a heavy ask. In college, she had been sure that she would eventually find a guy who understood that sometimes, just spending a night cuddled up in a blanket with no expectation (but the possibility) of more was on the horizon. But so far? No luck.

Her sister was after her to date more, insisting that it was a numbers game, and if she'd just download an app and start going to more business community functions, she'd find the perfect someone. Lydia liked to remind her that letting herself be swept up in romance wasn't all it was cracked up to be, after all. Trying to explain to Lydia that getting caught up in your emotions and making rash decisions wasn't the same as romance hadn't worked when she was 19, though, and it wasn't likely to work now.

Well, the business functions stuff wasn't a bad idea. She'd been active in the community when Small and Sparkling first launched, but she'd gotten so busy. Maybe the first activity for her assistant would be to see what upcoming events could fit into her schedule. As soon as he sorted out what the hell her schedule even was.

She could make her own coffee, if it came to it. Or give him private lessons.

No. Absolutely not. That is an example of the thought I am not going to have. That one right there.

"Okay. Are you free to do HR paperwork today?"

His smile spread wide, and her heart cracked open just a little bit.

As he went off to fill out an endless pile of forms and sign a million non-disclosure agreements, though, Olivia's mood took a nosedive. The rest of her day seemed almost insurmountably overwhelming. While the repair work from the morning's chaos had been delegated and was being completed, she still needed to oversee the patch jobs while also figuring out what the hell had happened and how to keep it from ever happening again. She was more than a little concerned that it had been her fault somehow. She'd green-lit something that wasn't ready or failed to double check a box. Blaming Callie wasn't fair. This was her position, and she needed to be able to keep up with it. The fate of her employees was resting heavy on her, and she wasn't sure how long she could hold it up.

She headed back to her office to pull up her email and look at the confusing, messy to-do list Callie had left her. She reordered the items in a way that made sense and then put them into her bullet journal. No one had ever understood this habit of hers, taking this part of her life and writing it down so that she could remember it more easily. She'd never had a problem with product schedules and project management being done with digital tools, but when it came to what she, personally, needed to get done in a day, writing it down with a series of dots and squares and decorating it with some colored pencils and washi tape settled down the part of her brain that was otherwise frantically trying to remember everything, in order, all the time.

Once she had the list written down, she reviewed it and, not for the first time, tried to figure out how she was going to get 20 hours of work done in 8. Closer to 7, now, since she'd spent her first hours of the day putting out fires and then hiring someone who, at least theoretically, could make it all a little easier to manage. Once he got up to speed, anyway, and who knew how long that would take? Who knew how long she could hold out, financially? How deep in the hole was she willing to go?

There was a light tap at her door and she looked up, trying to wipe the stress off her face and replace it with her friendly, professional smile. It was Callie standing there, and her friend didn't hold off for a second. She slipped into the office, closing the door behind her. "Okay, I was expecting to ask if you hired the hot eye candy for me to ogle, but something else is clearly happening. Spill."

Olivia couldn't keep the mask up. "I know we've been talking about how the numbers are down overall—token subscriptions, ad impressions, ad buys, all of it—but it's starting to add up now. I'm worried we're going to need to start laying people off."

Callie sank into the chair across from Olivia, puffing out her cheeks with a big breath. "It won't just be us. The boom is fading out for all of the tech companies, and everyone has to downsize. It's that or close. Have you been talking to accounting?"

"Yeah. They're giving me different projections and options on Thursday. Short of a genie in a bottle or a smash hit of a book that we don't actually have in the pipeline..." Her voice trailed off; she wasn't really sure what she was going to say next. Did all business owners feel like this, these responsibilities to the people they'd hired? Things had exploded for Small and Sparkling overnight, and they'd gotten her through it. She'd watched going viral destroy small companies when they were suddenly overwhelmed and unable to provide the service that had made them famous.

Callie was quiet for a long moment, and then asked, very quietly, "How much have you taken out of your savings?"

The fact that it was 'how much' and not 'have you' said a lot about her and about how much Callie understood her. "Not much. Enough. Enough that I can't do it indefinitely."

Callie blew out another long breath. "Liv. Laying off employees is not a moral failing. I know you. You're going to make sure they get unemployment, you're going to write glowing references for every single customer service rep, you're probably going to reach out to other people you know to see if they're hiring and are interested in taking first crack at whatever staff end up leaving."

It was all true. "I'm just worried, Callie. How far down will it go, you know? Is this the beginning of the end?" That was the real fear, underneath everything else. What if this was the start of watching her dream crumble into dust?

Callie knew her well enough to know that a bunch of meaningless platitudes wouldn't do anything. She just reached out, took Olivia's hand, and squeezed.

Chapter 6

Thomas

It was after lunch by the time he finished completing tax forms and signing what felt like a million different NDAs, policy acknowledgements, and receipt of various handbooks and guides. He'd also filled out reimbursement paperwork for a metro pass or a parking allowance. With all of that complete, Thomas was given logins for the various computer systems, a quick tour of the office, and then shown to his desk, which was logically right outside Olivia's office. Callie ran by, tossed him the manual for the computer programs he was expected to use and a quick start sheet for the phone system, and...that was what he got. No direction, no ideas about what Olivia would need assisting with, nothing. It made sense that he'd need to work that out with her, but...some guidance would have been a good start.

The desk he'd been shown to was a total disaster. The last guy had been fired about a month ago, he'd been told, but no one seemed to have cleaned up his desk. He wasn't sure how much order there had been before, but now, there was an ugly stew of paperwork that threatened to descend into complete chaos the second he breathed wrong. Okay. Clearly, cleaning up the desk was going to be his first step.

He was carefully pulling what looked like a paper calendar out from under a stack of message slips, many of which seemed to be less than a month old, when the phone rang next to him. He went to grab it, but before he could get his hand around the receiver, someone snatched it up. Olivia was standing over him, an inscrutable look on her face. "Small and Sparkling, Olivia Michaelson—" she paused, and Thomas could hear an indistinct voice speaking very quickly. "Yes, I know, still answering my own phone!" She gave an incredibly fake laugh, but he might not have caught it if he hadn't been watching her face and seen the tension in her eyes. The tension sharpened suddenly, and her lips parted in what looked concerningly like the beginnings of panic. "The meeting? I—" She looked at Thomas with wide eyes that were impatient and frustrated. He recognized those eyes. Those were just-before-finals eyes. He started flipping through the most recent messages, vaguely remembering something with today's date on it. He held it up, pointing to the item in blue pen that had been circled roughly a thousand times. *GENEVIEVE TAPAS 3:30.* Hopefully it was a code she would understand.

After a second, recognition lit up her face and she faked another laugh. "Of course I remember the meeting with Genevieve. I'm leaving the office now, remind me, is it the one on K street, or over on 17th? And do you already have a table?" He nodded at her, an affirmation of an executive-level save, as she finalized the details. As soon she hung up the phone, she darted into her office and emerged with a one of those leather backpacks that was designed to look very business-like and not at all like a backpack. He stood halfway up out of his chair. "Where are we going?" he asked, trying to figure out his next step.

She glanced back without stopping. "I'm going to see Genevieve, you're going to show me you can type something!"

She was far enough away that he had to call out to her. "What am I typing?"

The elevator opened, and she stepped inside. "Words!"

He couldn't quite tell if she was laughing when the door dinged shut, and Thomas sighed. No more great pleasure of fine eyes for now. He surveyed the chaos surrounding him. That had been a lucky save for both of them, and it was clear that this mess of a desk was behind at least some of it. Well, he'd read all the manuals and the training packets, and no one seemed particularly interested in the part of his job where someone explained what he was supposed to be doing. He did know one universal truth: that an office had a system. He knew systems, he just needed to figure out what this one was. He started looking over the scattered pages on his desk, absently typing the login information with one hand as he tried to decipher what someone meant when they drew a picture of a duck next to "PM Software" on the paper desk calendar that was three years old.

After an hour, he'd concluded that the duck was just a duck, and this office didn't have a system. He threw away the desk calendar, but kept the picture of the duck and taped it to the bottom of the computer monitor. It was an old computer science trick, having a duck (or some other inanimate object, but he'd always been fond of the classics) to bounce ideas off of when no one else was around, and he figured the duck could give him a hand as he started working his way through the life of Olivia. Which, as it turned out, was made significantly more difficult by apparent redundancies in meetings, "master lists" in three different places with three different sets of data, and a thousand other little things that were clearly bogging her down. At one point she appeared to have a meeting scheduled across town, in the office, in a different part of the office, and some-where in New Jersey. The project management software, which looked to be a free version of a program that he would have scoffed at three years ago and was currently so out of date that he was surprised it was still running at all, was only half-used and was used so differently by every department as to be irreconcilable. He saw at least three messages on the company chat program that read "Check your texts." He looked at the chaos in front of him, effectively what he and his classmates would have called spaghetti code, and did what any good programmer would do.

"Fredrick," he said to the duck, as that was apparently now the duck's name, "Sometimes the pipes in a system become so rusty they're not worth salvaging. We're going to start over now."

He started typing words, just as she'd asked, cross-referencing every direction Olivia was being yanked and smoothing out her schedule piece by piece. Since she walked into the conference room with her bound journal and her fate in his hands, Thomas had wanted to do innumerable things to that woman. For now, he would do this, and if he was very lucky, she would give him another one of those smiles that were definitely going to keep him up tonight.

Rebuilding her schedule was going to inherently up-end everything the company used for internal communications, so as he reorganized her life into something a person could actually live, he drafted a proposal for the different software replacements that would be useful and how to roll them out to the company at large. Since they weren't using any of the ones they currently had, he didn't feel like it would be an incredibly difficult switch.

By the end of the day, he wasn't sure that he had any real sense of what was going on at a broad picture level, but he was positive he knew what Olivia needed to be doing the next day. He needed to stop off at a stationery store on his way home from work for a couple things that would make everything a little easier. As everyone else around the office was grabbing their bags and heading for the doors, he pulled out his phone and dialed Abby, his little sister. "Hi," he said, once she answered. "I need to know more about bullet journaling." He cut off her squeal of delight with what was possibly the more important question. "And how many different ways are there to make coffee, anyway?"

Chapter 7

Olivia

When Olivia got to the office the next morning, she was in something approaching high spirits. Her meeting with Genevieve Starr—real name, Anne Nowak, but she'd often found it easier to use people's pennames for scheduling purposes so she could easily pull up their rankings and status when she was sitting down with them—had gone well. Anne's current story had been finished for a couple months, and she'd been dragging her heels a little on starting a new one. She'd finally come up with a new plot, but while her last several novels had been simple, slice-of-life contemporary stories, she wanted to take a run at a spy novel. She'd brought some samples with her, and they'd looked over them together. Olivia absolutely loved them. It was the female main character that was the super spy, and her blind date was the guy who got pulled into the adventure with her. Anne had gone home with an outline and a promise of the first 10,000 words in two weeks.

This was what she lived for. Too many authors felt pigeon-holed into writing what they'd always written. Once there were pages to look at, she and Anne would talk over how to transition her existing audience to the new story, but the beauty of Small and Sparkling was that the audience was often turning up for the experience rather than just the author, so convincing new people to read the story wasn't as hard as selling a stand-alone book in a traditional market. This was the part of her job she'd started to miss more and more.

She was surprised when she walked into the office and found Thomas already at his desk. Jackson had always gotten in on time, but he'd never once been early. The desk was spotlessly clean, as well. It looked like Thomas had tossed out that antique paper desk calendar and replaced it with a modern desk mat. The keyboard was absolutely not office issue. He had pen cup with what looked like an almost random assortment of pens and highlighters, and it made her laugh that she could identify some of them from six feet away. *A Pilot G2 man. Nice pick, Callie.* "Good morning," she said.

He looked up at her and flashed a grin that, if he tossed her one of those every morning, was going to be worth every cent of his salary. After a long night spent considering whether she could handle all the fantasy-worthy material that came with having an employee who was this damn physically affecting to her, she'd decided it was worth it. If nothing else, he could be the band playing on the deck of the Titanic as it sank. Callie was right; if everything went to hell, she would do everything she could to find her people new jobs. Including Mr. Gorgeous here.

She had no idea what it was about him. She didn't normally get this physically fascinated by someone; she usually needed to get to know them a little bit before finding her body tightening with anticipation just because they looked her way, and she'd certainly never had this kind of response to someone she hadn't kissed. Maybe this was what everyone meant when they talked about crushes. It certainly felt like the kind of infatuation that was always being tossed about in the novels she published. Whatever it was, she was enjoying the heady feeling, and it was a major relief from the crushing exhaustion and depression she'd been facing at work every day for the last—God, it felt like forever.

"Good morning," he responded, and she'd wandered so far into her own thoughts that she was almost surprised at his speaking. "Let me give you a few minutes to get your things settled, and then I'll be right in."

She mentally slapped her hand at the image that flashed through her mind. "Sounds good," she said. She went into her office, hung up her bag, got out her laptop and journal, and turned on her computer, kicking off her shoes and sitting down as Thomas walked in. He was balancing a few things; a tablet, two travel mugs, and a few slips of paper. He gestured carefully at the chair across from her desk.

"May I?"

She nodded, and he sat down carefully, placing the mugs on her desk before balancing everything out. And then she was quiet, waiting to see what he had in store for her.

He pulled out the tablet and started to scroll around. It brought back flickers of Callie glancing through her confused schedule and made her groan inwardly. Jackson had at least brought her a somewhat random stack of papers; the scrolling didn't help.

"Okay," he said, after a minute. "I spent some time last night going through your calendar and the different appointments in different places. I needed to get some things consolidated, and, with your permission of course, I need to make some phone calls to figure out where a couple of different meetings are actually happening because there were four possibilities listed in three places. I noticed that you had calls with two different authors scheduled at 11; if you can let me know which one is more urgent, I can reschedule the other. You've got some free time this afternoon, so hopefully that'll work fine for them. I also took some notes about the different programs and software that are being used across the company to manage items. I have some thoughts about how that could be more seamless for you, and I took the liberty of booking myself half an hour in your afternoon so that we can go over the possibilities, as well as how I can best assist you. I'll send you the proposal I wrote up so that you can mark up any questions you have before we sit down."

She had managed to keep her jaw from dropping onto her chest, but only barely. "Proposal?"

He tossed her that sunlight bright grin again and her knees went a little weak. "You wanted me to show you that I know how to type."

"I did. You're right." He was talking about office duties, why was that making her press her thighs together to ease the heat blooming there and force herself to listen to his voice instead of imagining the things he could be whispering in her ear. *Mmm, that's right. Just like that. Relax for me. Good girl.*

He was watching her way too closely, as if he could imagine what she was thinking. As if he might be thinking something along the same line.

"I made sure your electronic schedule is up to date and ready to go. But I made this for you as well." He passed her the slip of paper. It took a moment for her to recognize it as a to-do list, the kind designed as a sticker.

"What's this?" She made sure her tone was curious and managed to keep it from being breathy and giving away the desire that was ricocheting through her for no damn reason.

"Oh, my sister uses a bullet journal too. She's said before that a digital calendar is really useful on the go, but when she's actually sitting at her desk, having a physical record of what she's doing, and in a way where it's easy to add notes about different meetings or research results, is helpful. She sent me a picture of the way she set it up. I'm sure everyone handles this differently, but I wanted you to have it in case it's useful. If there's a different format you prefer, let me know—or if writing it down yourself is part of your process, let me know and I'll make sure there's a way it's easy for you to copy out of email." As he handed it over, his fingers brushed hers, and she couldn't contain the tiny gasp at the shock of the touch. His gaze was steady on hers, and she didn't know if the touch was intentional or not.

"And what about those?" She gestured towards the travel mugs. It was an excuse to pull her hand back. The little sheet was about as long as a journal page, but only a third as wide. She could stick it in on a blank page and take notes about the different meetings and such as they happened. It would make her entire day more seamless.

He glanced at the mugs. "Oh! Right, sorry. I don't know much about making coffee, but I stopped by a store on my way home, and was told that a French press is a pretty basic way to get started. I didn't know what type of roast you preferred, though, so I made a couple of different types. That's a Sumatra dark roast, and that one is a medium blend from a local roaster with 'fruity, chocolatey notes.'" The quotation marks around the flavors were clear. "I wasn't sure which you'd prefer, so I brought both in. There's almond milk, oat milk, and regular milk all in the office fridge, plus a couple different sugar options, so let me know what you need and I'll bring it in."

"Oat milk," she said. "Just a little bit. No sugar." Was this what it was like to have a real assistant? If so, she was never going without ever again. "And that medium roast sounds amazing."

"Perfect."

"What are you going to do with the other one?"

"Drink it myself." The smiles were going to be her undoing, she knew it without question. "From what I understand, it's time for me to start learning my way around a cup of coffee."

"Are you going to take notes on my favorite coffees?"

His eyebrows furrowed for just a moment, like she'd asked him if the sky was blue. "Yes?"

Oh. Oh, she was going to die. "I recommend the first few sips without any kind of creamer or sugar, then. It helps you understand the flavors of the coffee." She took a sip from the mug he'd indicated was the medium roast and then stopped herself from inviting him to try a sip.

"I'll do that," he said. He stood up, one hand in his pants pocket. She kept herself from admiring them, especially since his waist was basically at eye level, and glancing down just a little would be perfectly natural. "Let me know about the phone call so I can make the appropriate adjustments. I'm still getting the hang of the phones, but I'll try to screen calls for you. And just let me know what you need."

He nodded to her and walked away. She enjoyed every single second of the view so much that she had to snap her eyes back up when he turned to look at her again. "Door open or closed?"

"Open, for now." There was a little sparkle in his eyes at her answer. If she'd told him to close it, which side of the door would he have put himself on? Was he actually flirting with her?

"You got it, boss."

She sat frozen in place for a long moment. She never sat in a chair like a normal person, with both feet on the floor, but when she finally shifted to curl one leg up under her, she had to immediately put her foot down again. It would be far too easy to put all those yoga classes to work and press her heel into that delicious and almost painful heat that was wide awake in her core. Those thoughts were not work appropriate. None of this was work appropriate.

He was younger than her, and he reported to her. It was not possible for there to be a less equal power dynamic. But she would put actual money down on a bet that he was actually flirting with her.

She could think her way around the age gap without too much difficulty. He was an adult, and well into the age of reason. He could make his own choices about that. But the work thing, even looking at him wrong could be considered sexual harassment. He wasn't just forbidden fruit, he was sirens-blaring off-limits fruit. Maybe she did need to start going on some dates. Wanting to have some romance in her life was all well and good, but if she was reacting this hard to a brush of fingers, like she was the heroine in a historical novel where showing off her ankles could cause a scandal, she really did need more sex in her life. Clearly, her vibrator was not doing the job well enough.

Chapter 8

Thomas

Thomas seriously wished that Olivia had asked for the door to be closed. He wanted more than anything to lean back on it and draw a long, steadying breath like a character in a movie. Instead, he kept his hand in his pocket, pulling his pants forward to try and disguise the fact that all the concentration and focus in the world hadn't been able to keep him from getting a little hard after the way Olivia had looked at him: like a candy she wanted to unwrap and pop in her mouth. He'd finally managed to find out what the last assistant had done to get fired, and while pitching a tent while talking to your boss was always going to be at least a little gauche, after that mess he wouldn't have blamed anyone in the building from tarring and feathering him before kicking him out of the seventh floor windows if lingering looks lasted a little too long.

He sat down at his desk and tried to get himself under control. Long, deep breaths. Unsexy things. He couldn't think of unsexy things, he could only think of kissing her to find out what that coffee tasted like on her lips.

He was no stranger to wanting someone, although he didn't usually find himself drawn this hard and so fast. In any other situation, given the way she was reacting to him, he wouldn't have hesitated to claim there was something at the corner of her mouth and reached across the desk to brush his thumb over her lower lip. He wouldn't have hesitated to be the one who encouraged the next step, to making it a delight for someone to say yes, to showing them how very good they could feel. And in all honesty, he wasn't sure that the fact that she was his boss would have stopped him, given how strong his desires were. But her sheer level of nerves was more than enough to make him hold back. Sometimes, a person was looking for an excuse to say yes. Sometimes they were afraid to. In that first situation, he was very good at providing opportunities, but in the second...he wasn't interested in pushing past limits that a person might regret, in the moment or later.

But none of that was keeping him from imagining moving around the desk, lifting her to her feet, and pressing her up against the window and the gorgeous view while he found out exactly what she tasted like.

He kept his groan internal, did his best to be subtle as he adjusted himself, and went back to work transferring information from a couple dozen completely random spreadsheets into a useful database. He'd pulled down the free version of the software, but based on the professional membership fees she was paying, she would be able to get a code to upgrade it with a couple of emails. He had around five hours between now and when he had scheduled their meeting. He could get himself under control by then.

About three seconds after he walked into the office that afternoon, however, he knew he absolutely did not have control of himself. Olivia had told him not to worry about coming to meetings with her until he had his feet under himself, so he spent the day learning the phones, putting together lists of people who were likely to call her and sorting them into "put through immediately," "put through if possible," and "I'm so sorry, she's in a meeting, I'll have her get back to you." He'd only seen her when she was rushing from place to place, and while it was a nice view, he had been able to keep his hormones in check.

I got cocky, he thought, only appreciating the irony after a moment. *I somehow forgot what I was looking at.*

When Olivia had walked into that conference room, he'd thought she was beautiful. Currently, she was leaning over a tablet that was placed on top of her keyboard, her cheeks resting on her hands. A stylus was in her fingers and she was tapping it in rhythm on the top of her head. In short, she was frustratingly adorable. He was such a sucker for adorable.

In some distant part of his brain, he was aware that he was reacting very strongly to someone he'd met just over 24 hours ago. If he'd met her when he was at a party or out with Mason, he'd probably still be deciding whether he wanted to call her and ask her out. But she was here, and in front of him, and not just beautiful. She was adorable.

And smart. And funny. And dedicated to what she was doing. And his dick would not keep calm around her. He kept his laptop in front of him like a goddamned teenager and cleared his throat.

She jerked her head up like a kid who'd gotten caught doing something naughty. "Sorry! I didn't mean to keep you waiting."

"Not a problem," he said, sitting down across from her and opening up his laptop. "So did you have a chance to look over what I sent?"

"I did," she said. "Impressive work."

He laughed. "Thank you."

"First day of work and you're rewriting everything about my company's procedures. Ballsy." Her tone was different now than it had been. She wasn't unprofessional, but that veneer of propriety was gone. Her voice sounded softer. Like it would be easier to make her laugh.

"You hired me to assist you," he said, trying to match her light tone. "I'm assisting."

"So, tell me what I'm looking at here."

"Basically, you're working with software that you probably set up when the company had—what, maybe 50 employees?" She nodded. "And then you just kept tacking on more software that would do the things you needed it to." Another nod. "Okay. So that probably worked great when everyone was working within a stone's throw of each other, but now, with different department heads in different areas of the offices, a huge amount of your workforce remote or hybrid, it's not working as well. There aren't any real defined rules about how different data is being categorized or handled, so every department is doing it differently. It's impossible to organize. The best solution is to tear it all down and start over. Retraining people on a new program is actually more effective than trying to patch how they use an old one because you don't have to break bad habits." Talking about computers was requiring him to engage his logical brain, which was making his dick settle down, which he appreciated.

"I understand what you're saying," she said. "But the company doesn't have the funds necessary to invest in brand new software right now. I appreciate this—"

"Oh, that's the beauty of it," he cut in. "You're a member of the Women Business Owners of the Metropolitan Area group, right?"

"Yes."

"Their members are entitled to a free pro account on the software I mentioned. You just have to email..." he glanced at the document he had up on his screen.

"Dorothy Yardley. She'll give you the code. They even offer a free webinar to teach the basics of the software."

She nodded. "Okay. But tell me about the app?"

"That's more of a question, really," he said. "Why doesn't Small and Sparkling have an app?"

She sighed and rubbed her temples. "There are a bunch of reasons. All of the microfiction sites have one, and I know there's a lot of engagement on them, but I've never come up with anything that would differentiate us from the other options out there. If we're just another platform offering the same things, is it worth it?"

"But you're not offering the same things. Your entire product line is different, and the UI would reflect that. You'd set it up to mirror the website, make sure the branding was consistent, and build in the functionality that would suit you best."

She shook her head. "Either way. We don't have the money to develop it, so I don't see the point in thinking about it."

There were a million thoughts in his head about growth and expansion and opportunities, but ultimately, those were Mason's field, not his. He was the idea guy, the coding guy. Mason was the convince-the-client-to-do-it guy.

"Thank you though, truly. You may be right about the software. I'm going to do some reading about this, maybe get in touch with..." she glanced at the document. "Dorothy." Then she leaned back, studying him and smiling. "You've got some pretty nice typing skills."

She made it sound absolutely filthy, and all that computer-based calm drained directly out of him. Was she aware of the effect she was having on him? The smile she wore was casual and calm, not the look he expected to see when someone had sex on the mind and the will to work for it. *Stop thinking about what she'd look like when she was working for it.* No, she was just being friendly.

It didn't matter if she was doing it on purpose or not right now. This was untenable. He'd been half hard for 24 hours, even after he'd stroked himself raw last night. This woman was turning him inside out, and if she somehow didn't know it, then she needed to know it.

"I'm sorry," he said, and pushed as much truth into the tone as he could. He was sorry. What he was about to do would be considered to be very awkward by some people, and borderline illegal by others. "I need to clarify something."

"What's that?" Her eyes were wide, and her mouth was open just the tiniest bit.

"The way you're talking, smiling at me, looking at me. Do you know you're doing it?"

Her eyebrows shot up, but she didn't say anything.

He put his hands up. "Look, signals can be misread and misunderstood. Maybe you make comments to all your employees about their typing skills. If I'm making you uncomfortable, I'll go. I'm not interested in being threatening or causing problems for you. God knows I don't want you to think of me like you probably think of the last guy."

The sudden flush that spread across her cheeks did not make his erection easier to control.

"So, I just need to know what you consider to be appropriate. I want to make sure I stay within the lines and don't cause problems. And if I'm not what you want to have here, I'll go." He smiled a little and let it go just a touch wolfish. "Though if you told me to go, I'd want to know if I could ask you out as I left. So, tell me. What do you think is appropriate right now?"

Chapter 9

Olivia

Olivia was pinned in place by her own indecision. He was absolutely right, she'd been flirting mercilessly with that last comment, and she was completely out of line. But she was also exactly where she wanted to be. Saying that out loud, though? That was beyond dangerous. It felt like a betrayal of everything she said she dreamed of. Elizabeth Bennet wasn't swept away by emotion; she was careful and considered. Her little sister had gotten caught up in lust and need and had almost been ruined by it.

What did she think was appropriate right now? His hands in her hair, him pressing her up against the desk, all the different ways that she could think of for him to make sparks fly behind her eyes. That was the most appropriate, the most right thing she could imagine.

"Stand up," he said, and she did it without thinking. There was a tone in his voice that made her want to listen to him, make her want to hear him. He stood too, and she realized then what had made him react like this. His erection was clear and harsh against his slacks. She wondered if he'd been feeling like this all day. She had. The fact that it was easier to hide didn't mean she hadn't spent most of the day trying to come up with a reason for him to come into her office just so she could look at him again.

She didn't realized she'd looked her lips while getting an eyeful of his cock until she heard the small sound he made. Somewhere between a grumble and a growl.

"I'm going to walk toward you now," he said. His voice was soft and slow, careful. "If you want me to stop, just hold up your hand. All you have to do is say stop, or no, or anything even close to it, and I'll go. I won't make a fuss, you can tell Callie I was just bad at the job, and I'll tell Mason the same thing. No harm, no foul." He took slow, careful steps toward her. Around the desk and toward her. It was about five steps, and he took each one with a precision that made heat spool out of her belly into her limbs and her breasts and between her thighs. And then he was standing directly in front of her, maybe a hand span away. "Is this appropriate? Olivia?"

He said his name like he was already kissing her. She couldn't bring herself to say anything.

"It's up for debate, I suppose. I can hear you better when I'm this close. See you better, too. From this distance, I could even kiss you." She couldn't control the little sound that came out of her throat, the tiniest whimper ever. It made him smile. "But you're my boss, Olivia. If you want me to kiss you, I'm going to need you to ask me to." He chuckled. "With actual words. So, there's no misread signals, no confusion."

She looked up to meet his eyes and tell him that he was being wildly inappropriate, that he should leave the office immediately and not come back. She'd call Callie in and tell her to do what they should have done a month ago and call a temp agency. She should banish this man, this much younger man, from her mind and get on with running her business and figuring out her life.

But then she thought of two coffee mugs on her desk this morning. What had he said? That he wasn't sure which roast she preferred, so he'd made both? He'd gone home and, presumably, learned to make coffee for her. *To be a better assistant.* That was horseshit. A good assistant asked where her favorite coffee shop was, bought coffee on the way to work, and expensed it to the company at the end of the week. There was more to it than that.

To make that thought disappear, she found the best way she could think of to distract herself. She placed her hand on his chest, convinced she was going to push him away. But then she was up on her toes and kissing him.

His hands came to her waist and held her, but not to crush her to him. His mouth, however, was not as restrained. He didn't kiss her particularly hard, but he kissed her thoroughly, his mouth moving over hers and his tongue teasing at her lower lip until she opened for him. The one hand had stayed on his chest, but the other slipped up around his neck to pull him down to her. He tasted amazing, sweet and like chocolate. His tongue brushed through her mouth and claimed her in a way that she wasn't sure she would ever recover from. Her fingers tightened harder on the back of his neck, and he made a sound low in his throat, his hands pulling her closer.

And she panicked. There were no other words for it; she panicked and stepped back, out of his reach and out of his grasp. Her knees were shaking, and she tried desperately to keep herself under control. She didn't know the last time she had needed anyone—anything— as much as his mouth on hers, his body pressing up against her, something making this heat spiral up into an explosion.

The door to her office was open, and even if it wasn't, she wasn't going to do this here. For a moment, she latched onto the idea of a date. Fire him, then ask him out on a date. That was good for office morale, wasn't it?

"There," she said, trying and failing to keep her voice steady. "I think we've both gotten that out of our sys- tems." Like she wasn't gasping for air and his cock wasn't somehow straining at his pants even harder than it had been. "I have a...a late meeting outside the office, and I don't want to be late. I forgot to put it on the sched- ule. So, you can leave when you're ready. And I'll see you tomorrow!" She tried to make that last word sound chipper, and not like she was running away. Because that was, without question, what she was doing. Running away. She loaded her laptop into her bag and rushed out the door without looking behind her. She didn't want to know how he was looking at her. She didn't want to know what he was thinking.

As she stepped into the elevator, her heart was slamming against her ribs. She'd never been so...so un-thinking. She spent the descent to the ground floor enumerating her sins. The forbidden fruit concept was getting tired, obviously that didn't matter to her brain or her body. But she'd let him take control like that. She'd let him wake up a kind of need and awareness that she'd tended to disregard. The sensations of need and lust led to nothing good, in her experience. She wanted a relationship, something more than just sex, and in her experience, starting from sex had never led to the kind of emotional connection she wanted. Her grandmother would have said something disgustingly sexist, like 'why buy the cow when you can get the milk for free,' and she'd never seen it like that. The fault was almost certainly on her end. Her inability to let go, her inability to find the connections she wanted.

The elevator dinged at the lobby and her time for feeling guilty was over. She did her best to shake it off like a dark cloud and headed toward the metro, and home.

Once she was safe in her own house and had set up her elaborate siphon coffee maker for an evening cup – decaf, of course, since she wanted to sleep tonight, and long gone were the days where she could drink caffeine after 3pm and not be awake until dawn—she finally allowed herself to slow down and process what had happened in that office. Thomas was incredibly attractive. He was tall, and while he wasn't bulky like a superhero, he had the strong, solid look of a guy who lifted weights but also ate a balanced diet instead of ridiculous amounts of protein smoothies. His hair was the perfect length to sink your fingers into, and his eyes, she'd discovered, had that 'stare deep into your soul' quality that made her shiver with pleasure. So, it made sense that she'd been overwhelmed by him for a moment.

It was the timeframe, at this point, that was making her squirm with discomfort. She'd met this man less than two days ago, but if he'd pressed his advances at all...she didn't even want to think about what she would have been willing to do there, in her office with her door open. What she would have said yes to, with the most enthusiastic consent she could possibly manage. That just wasn't like her. Or at least, it wasn't like who she wanted to be.

She pulled out her laptop and her bullet journal to see what she needed to do tonight, after leaving work hours early because she couldn't keep her hormones under control. The to-do list pasted into her journal, though, sent another little frisson of delight up her spine. She tried to shake it off—who got turned on by stationery? —but she couldn't, not entirely. There was something there about how quickly he'd assessed her, figured out what she needed, made sure she had it. Sweet and kind and generous. He'd brought her two cups of coffee to see which she liked better after showing no signs of even knowing what a pour over or a French press was less than 24 hours previous.

She pushed her attention off the delicate purple sticker and onto what had actually been written on it. The penmanship was tidy, all block capitals and written in a black ink that looked like it would hold up to a highlighter, if necessary, which meant he'd branched out from his Pilot G2 stockpile.

No. She was not giving him extra emotional credit just for being a good assistant. She had shit to do.

With a solid effort, she looked at the next item on the list, which had been organized in an incredibly good approximation of priority, and got to work.

Chapter 10

Thomas

Thomas lay flat on his bed, staring at the ceiling, trying to think about literally anything in the world other than how incredibly good it had felt when Olivia's mouth opened under his. How his mind had played through a thousand versions of what could have come next, from teasing her nipples and her clit until she was gasping into his shoulder to muffle her cries as she came—he thought she might be a screamer, though he wasn't sure she knew it—to shutting the door and fucking her right there. Instead, she'd panicked and ran, leaving him to figure out how to calm down his raging cock enough that he could walk back to his desk and breathe through the blinding lust.

He groaned as his cock stiffened again. He'd already stroked himself raw, but his body would not shut up about what it wanted. And what it wanted, clearly, was Olivia Michaelson. Who, quite clearly, was interested in him, but not interested in him enough to cross whatever line she'd placed in her head. The boundary she'd obviously placed around him was fair and her right to set. All that was left was for him to deal with it.

He was fairly sure that if he walked into the living room and told Mason that the job wasn't working out, that he wasn't cut out for it, Mason would shrug and tell him that what he did was up to him. He'd still be able to stay here, still look for a job that would get him started, and he'd be able to cruise the freelance scene and look for something that way. It wasn't right to stay at Sweet and Sparkling with the way he was feeling. With how much he wanted her every time he looked at her.

But the thing was that it wasn't just lust, not really. It was the surprise and banked happiness she'd shown when he pulled out her coffee options. It was the shock when he'd handed her the sticker list for her bullet journal. It was the amount of surprise she was showing at someone presenting her with what he considered the most basic amount of human consideration, even beyond someone who was being paid to, quite literally, assist her.

He didn't want to quit the job. The woman he'd met in that conference room was beautiful, tugged at something deep inside of him, and ultimately, he just thought she was a person he'd get to liking. But beyond that, there was something rotten in the state of Small and Sparkling. Or, more specifically, it's complete lack of a system. One of the reasons he'd fallen in love with programming early on was the magic of the compile. Of taking all the disparate pieces and random, broken strings of English and watching their grammar and sense emerge as they created something unique and exciting. Coding was artwork, and he'd happily fight anyone who said it wasn't. It was just as creative as novel writing or painting, and he'd happily put a smoothly functioning, bug-free app with a user-friendly UI up against the Mona Lisa any day.

Going through the insane piles of notes, weird calendar systems, and uncoordinated spreadsheets had been like finding a skein of yarn on the floor after a cat had gotten into it. Tangled, damp, bitten through in places...but still something useful in the guts of it. There was something at the heart of Small and Sparkling, and if he could tease it out, the entire place could run efficiently, neatly, productively, and well. He liked putting the universe in order.

So, staying at the job would let him scratch his itch to tidy up some of the randomness in the universe, help a pretty woman make her day a little easier, and also start to shore up his dwindling bank account. He couldn't think of a downside.

His cock decided that was the moment to give a little twitch, a potent reminder that Olivia Michaelson was deep under his skin, and that one small taste of her hadn't "gotten that out of his system," to paraphrase her. All he wanted was more. But she didn't want it, and he wouldn't press. He'd do his job. And find a way to keep his dick under control.

Somehow.

***

By Friday, Thomas felt like he was finally starting to get the hang of the whole assistant drill. The morning after their ill-fated make-out session, Olivia had told him to go ahead with basic setup for the project management software he'd laid out for her. Whether it was because she thought it was a good idea or because she was horrified to look at his face and see what she'd done, he wasn't sure. It didn't matter too much. He still got to live the dream of making life easier for her and untangling the redundant, complicated, frustrating mess that her company had become without her knowing it. He'd gotten the basics of the software set up and created simple training documents that could be used throughout the company to help make sure that everyone was entering information the same way.

The project he'd started today was creating an author database. He'd been quizzing Olivia about what information she needed to access most easily and was setting up it up accordingly. Author's legal name, any other name they used personally, their pronouns, the different pen names they used, what genres those pen names were associated, links to the most recent financial and interaction reports for their work, connections to their specific editor, if their stories were eligible for inclusion in the monthly print edition, and a hundred other small details that Olivia would be able to have at her fingertips whenever she needed to deal with a specific author. Like the project management software, he knew it would be useful for everyone in the company, but making sure that it was universally useful wasn't his entire goal. That said, he was pretty sure that he could spend a few minutes with the company's barebones web development team and find a way to give authors better access to their own numbers.

He'd also found one item to track that was better to maintain as a purely analog system—though he'd die before he'd admit that to his sister. With a series of tally marks on different pages of a small spiral notebook, he was tracking the correlation between when someone asked a "quick question," a "super quick question," and a "do you have a minute?" question and how long it took for the question to be actually answered. He'd realized a long time ago that "quick questions" were absolutely never quick, but he'd been surprised that super quick questions, on average, took longer to answer than regular ones. They often involved research projects. If someone asked if Olivia "had a minute" later that day, he looked for an hour-long block of time. He'd been surprised to find that authors had a better sense of how long their questions were going to take to answer than other employees, but the data didn't lie.

The phone rang, and he picked it up smoothly. He hadn't bobbled the handset in two days, a miracle all on its own. "Hello?"

"Well, I finally get to talk to a person, isn't that nice?" The tone was so laced with sarcasm that Thomas felt his spine prickle and had to take a moment to avoid leaping into a sarcastic response.

"I'm glad to be the one you get to talk to!" He pushed cheer into his voice. He had somehow mentally missed the part where he would be spending so much time taking phone calls from irritated authors at this job. When programmers spent time talking to end users, it usually meant something had seriously broken down somewhere in the process. Companies had whole entire project managers for that sort of thing. "May I ask who's calling?"

"This is Jenny Lawson. Olivia was supposed to call me back several days ago about a serious error that was made in the publication of my story."

Something about the name tickled the back of his brain, but he couldn't place it. He searched for her name in his brand-new database, but he'd only gotten to G, so she wasn't there yet. One of the various handwritten notes on the desk? He started pulling out drawers and peering through notes he hadn't yet dropped into the circular filing system. Nothing. "I'm sorry she hasn't gotten back to you. Is there something I can help you with?"

The author gave a huge huff. "There was a major issue with my editor this week, and I need assurances that this kind of mistake won't happen again. Very small errors can make very big differences, and I'm still dealing with upset readers on my social media."

He glanced toward Olivia's door, but it was still closed. Her schedule had her blocked off for a phone call with an author they were trying to recruit. "I'm so sorry that you're having to deal with that." His customer service voice sucked, and he hoped he wasn't sounding dismissive. "We're working on rolling out some new tools that will make the entire editing process easier for you, and to improve our project management internally to avoid any complications in the future. What you went through was totally unacceptable." He hoped that was true, and he wasn't expressing some weird position that would end up costing Olivia time and resources. "I'm just glad that I could resolve the problem at all," Lawson said, her tone somewhat mollified. "I can't imagine the consequences if this had happened to an author without my ability to bounce back. Someone new at this could have really suffered, and I know that Olivia wouldn't want that on her conscience."

"You're right, of course." He hoped.

"What are these new tools you're talking about?"

He should have anticipated that question, but he hadn't, and he stumbled over his response. ""Which ones are you wondering about?"

"All these different ways to get in touch with editors, with promotions. Why is it all suddenly more complicated?"

He was quietly miffed at the suggestion. He'd spent plenty of time making sure he was implementing the most user-friendly tools he could find without breaking into Small and Sparkling's limited budget. "Well, the goal definitely isn't to make it more complicated. I know that it has sometimes been hard to access people in administration, and we want to simplify that process—"

"Maybe it is for some people." He was a little shocked the woman didn't say ""whippersnappers." Her voice didn't sound old, but her tone certainly did. "But not all writers have the most up-to-date programs or the most tech savvy backgrounds. I do fine, but some of the others in the Discord are really struggling, and the rest of us are helping out as best as we can't. I'd think you would have included some how-to manuals along with all these new programs."

He had written how-to manuals. Well, one-sheets. He opened a new note on his desktop and, typed "References??" so he wouldn't forget to find out why those hadn't gone out along with the author invitations. Now, he had a bigger question, however. "What Discord?" If there was yet another communication tool that someone had forgotten to tell him about, he thought he might pull out his hair. He'd gotten Mason to lay off with the wax, too, so it would be much easier to grip.

Now Lawson sounded a little like the kid who'd gotten their hand caught in the cookie jar. "The Discord server that we authors set up for ourselves. To talk about what was going on with the company, since no one there seemed particularly interested in sharing the information with us directly."

Well, shit, that wasn't a good sign at all. Yet another thing to bring up with Olivia. "I see. I wonder if it would be helpful for us to incorporate some kind of server like that in the new chat program. I'll raise the issue and make sure that it gets reviewed."

He'd thought that would ease the author's concerns, but instead of calming down, she sounded a bit more on edge. "I don't know why there's this sudden push towards making everything so much more...corporate. Part of the appeal of Small and Sparkling has always been how approachable everything is. All these layers between people just feels...wrong."

This one he'd talked out with Olivia, at least to a certain degree, so he felt more comfortable with the spin. "I can see how it feels that way." Lawson snorted, but he kept going. "All I can do is promise you that we're making every effort to simplify things. I know it can take some getting used to, but I'm sure that once things settle down and people are used to the new system, it will be much easier to communicate, and that will help avoid issues like the one you had." Whatever it was. And, hey, genius plan. "I know the phone tree can be a pain in the ass, also, so let me give you the number directly to my desk, just in case anyone runs into problems that seem excessive." He rattled off the number and hoped that Lawson was both writing it down and not horribly offended.

"Fine," she said, and he was very afraid she'd landed on the latter option. Well, fuck. "Thank you for your time. And I still want to hear from Olivia, as soon as she can reach out to me."

"I'll make sure to let her know. Thank you for reaching out."

There was a final 'hmph" before the call disconnected.

Thomas threw his head back like someone crossing the finish line after a marathon and thanking God they hadn't dropped dead halfway through. When he came back to a normal sitting posture, he found himself face to face with Callie. She was giving him a smile of solidarity, and it occurred to him that she had been just around the corner at the beginning of that phone call. "Everything good?" she asked.

"Yeah, fine," he said. "Not all the authors are completely excited about the new contact options. I'd've thought that writers would be much happier getting to write down their concerns instead of needing to actually get on the phone and talk to people. "I'm sure they'll catch up," she said. And then turned on her million-watt smile. Not for the first time, he wondered why she and Mason weren't together. She was exactly his type: small, perky, blonde, and brilliant. He knew she'd gone to school for graphic design, and her school had been relatively close to theirs, so distance wasn't an issue. He couldn't find out about any random falling out that would have left lingering difficulties, and neither one of them was shy about who they dated, when, or how much. When he'd tried to hint around the subject, Mason had changed it. When Thomas tried the classic "what if I ask her out" gambit, he got a shrug and a "go for it, she's a great girl." But there had been something tense in Mason's tone when he said it, keeping Thomas from believing that his friend was really as distant from the idea of Callie dating other people as he might want people to think. It was a mystery; a bit of weird code didn't fit into the overall program. He couldn't figure it out, and it was only more confusing as he was getting to know Callie in the office. "So, I have a quick question," she said, and he had to hold back a burst of laughter. Thus far, her quick questions hadn't been incredibly long ones, but they fit the pattern of "definitely not actually quick." She must have noticed the look on his face, because this time she was the one trying not to laugh. "It really is a quick one this time though."

That's what everyone thinks. He didn't know his co-worker/boss's best friend/his best friend's best friend well enough to say it out loud, but he thought it very hard. "What can I do for you?"

"I know you're not actually my assistant, but if you have time, can you help me set up a meeting with Alyssa Orville? I need to get some confirmation from her about layouts before I can finalize the print issue for this month, but she's working remote for the next two weeks and I'm having the worst time trying to get ahold of her."

"Do you know if she's set up in the new systems yet?" He spun toward his monitor and started typing, looking to see if she'd accepted one of the invitations that had been sent out. Nope.

"I don't think so. She's really bad about her email, so she might not even know what's up."

He added "author and client nudge" underneath "how-to manuals" on his list. "Maybe try sending her the invite through her cell? I can try and get ahold of her, too."

"Thanks," Callie said. "You know, I wonder how all these changes look from the outside."

Jenny Lawson had certainly seemed to find them concerning. "Why do you ask?"

"Just thinking that these are all big changes for our authors, and they're happening really fast. I hope it doesn't look like we're losing focus on what matters."

He studied her carefully, but it didn't look like she was trying to be weird or passive aggressive with her comment; it was just an observation.

"Thomas?"

Olivia's voice caught his attention and he turned toward it without hesitation. "What can I do for you?"

"I need a hand," a sharp pause in her words, followed by "assistance," with a little extra emphasis, "with a scheduling issue."

He allowed himself one moment to luxuriate in the thought of her needing his hands, then focused on what he was here to do. "Of course." He stood up and flashed a quick smile at Callie. "Unless there's anything else I need to take care of here first?"

Callie glanced up from her phone. "Nope, I'm good. Alyssa actually just texted me back to let me know she's setting up the program and ask if we can meet in 15 minutes. Go work your miracles for her." She jerked her chin toward Olivia's door, and her voice lowered conspiratorially. "Get that growl in your voice under control, though. You sound like you want to devour her." He didn't know what look crossed his face, but Callie started to laugh, walking away and tapping on her phone.

Okay. He took five seconds to collect himself before walking through the door "I'm happy to help," he said in the most professional tone he had and was rewarded with a smile.

Chapter 11

Olivia

Olivia looked over the meeting notes that Thomas had compiled for her. She'd finally sat down with Callie, her head of finance, and the leader of the customer service team. She'd obfuscated the reason for the meeting—trying to figure out how to increase the company's overall revenue—by talking about what needs the readers might have that weren't being needed. The odds of finding a quick fix at this point were beyond tiny, but if she could find something that would probably work within six months, she could probably hold out, especially if she took out a small business loan. Once Thomas had pointed out the licensing option for that software he liked, she'd taken a closer look at the membership perks that came along with the various dues she paid. They included low interest loans for women-, LGBTQIA-, disabled-, and POC-owned businesses, as well as introductory meetings with angel investors.

The idea of an investor scared her. Small and Sparkling was her baby, and the idea of letting someone else have equity in the business made her shake a little inside. If someone else had a say in what happened, would she have the same freedom to focus on the stories she loved, or would she start needing to press into the territory of more erotic stories. It would bring in money, and fast, she knew, but it would dilute her brand hopelessly. The authors she loved, the ones she had been promoting for years, would get drowned out by the alpha shifter bad boy forced proximity stories that she privately enjoyed, but that were easy enough to find in the world. The story where the romance between the alpha shifter bad boy was the focus instead of the relationship specifically with his rippling abs and 12 inch cock, that was the story she wanted to see in the world. The one that tended to get squeezed out. She wanted to hold space for that story. Would an investor let her do that?

She pressed the heels of her hands into her eyes, vaguely wondering if the pressure would let her see differently enough to find the answer.

She wouldn't be able to get a loan for a business that was clearly losing money without a clear plan for how she could turn it around. She just needed a plan.

She looked up at the tap at her door. She shouldn't have been surprised to see Thomas there, but her heart still skipped a beat all the same. He'd been nothing but professional since that glorious kiss, and she'd made sure not to accidentally flirt anymore. He was still experimenting with coffee roasts and brew methods, and she was pretty sure he was taking notes on her opinions about the different options he brought her. He'd been adjusting her to-do lists based on what she prioritized. He'd been carefully getting her feedback as he got the project management software up and running, customizing it to her needs. When she had suggested that he should focus on the needs of the employees at large, he'd shaken his head. "Their needs are diverse and huge. We'll get to them later. You're the head of the company. The business's logic has to flow from your thought process. We'll help them find a way to work within it." He said 'we' a lot. Like he expected to stay around for a long time. Somehow, she hadn't expected that.

"Hey," she said. "What's up?"

"I wondered if you have any questions about the notes from the meeting. I thought I could clarify if I missed anything and then head out."

"Sure," she said. He nodded and started to turn away. The word 'wait' surprised her when she heard herself say it.

He turned back to her, eyebrows raised and his entire body attentive. Something about it reminded her of the way he'd walked—stalked—toward her before giving her the filthiest, most wonderful, toe-curling kiss she'd ever experienced. If she asked him to come and kiss her again, would he?

No. He wouldn't. They were going to be appropriate. That was perfectly clear now. She was going to act like an adult who was controlled by her brain instead of her clit.

She stumbled for a second, trying to find words to say that weren't sexual. "I was looking over your notes," she said, "and on the written out version, you wrote 'app' and circled it about a million times. What was that?"

That mask of professionalism shifted back into place in a heartbeat. It had probably been nothing but her own imagination anyway. "Mind if I sit?"

"No, of course," she said, her thighs trembling just a little as her brain replayed earlier events for her consumption. And the office was probably empty now anyway...

Stop. It.

"What did you want to know about it?"

"You think an app could help. Why?"

Thomas nodded and took a minute to consider his words. His thoughtful face was fascinating. His attention focused inward, his mouth pursed a little, and then, when he figured out what was going to come next, the corner of his mouth tilted up just the tiniest amount. "So, web novels got huge in East Asia, right? Their focus is on apps that can push updates," she must have looked just a little bit confused because he shifted his tone seamlessly and without a hint of condescension, "sending notifications to readers when a new chapter is updated. They can tap into it on their phone and read it on their commute to work. The online format is great, and it's regularly used, but an app expands the user base. More people have a smartphone than a computer, and there are more places you can read on your phone. In the bath, outside, in..." He trailed off and cleared his throat, carefully not looking at her.

She laughed, and she could hear the low tone in it that meant she was painfully close to being a flirt again. "You can say bedroom. We have various levels of heat for a reason."

He still didn't look at her. "It's just harder to read in bed with a laptop while your hands are busy."

She nodded. "It makes sense. Practically everyone else in the market has an app. But I've never been able to figure out what would make my app different from everyone else's. There's no point in just being another copy." He started to say something, but her words were flowing, and apparently there was no stopping the torrent. "Besides, they take serious capital to develop, and they take time. We don't..." she stopped herself from saying "have either one." She took a long, steadying breath. "It's a lot to do without a guarantee of return, you know? Our userbase skews a bit older than average, so there might be fewer people who want to use an app."

"That's another piece of it, though," he added. "A mobile app might bring in a younger crowd that is more comfortable with microtransactions."

She waved it off. It wasn't enough, it couldn't happen fast enough, and there was no point in discussing it further. He stopped talking, but his jaw worked for a moment, and she knew he had more he wanted to say.

"Thanks for clarifying the point," she said, pulling out the very best boss voice that she had. "It helps me to understand what's going on. I think I can sort out the rest without you. Go home, get some rest."

He studied her for a moment and then gave an abrupt nod. "See you on Monday."

Was it Friday? It was. Shit. When had that happened? Somewhere between one financial panic attack and another, she supposed. With one soul-searing kiss in between. "See you on Monday."

She was both relieved and disappointed when he walked out of the office without looking back.

She turned back to her notes and willed them to give her some new piece of information that would make it all fall together in her head. There was a path forward here. If she concentrated enough, she would find it.

But concentration was apparently not happening now. The ring on her cell phone made her jump, and she bobbled it for a moment before accepting the call and getting it up to her ear. "Lydia," she said, "You're early."

Her younger sister laughed. "You're still at work, aren't you?"

"Yes. That's why you're early."

"No, that's why you're working late again. Or at least, that's how I know you're working late again."

Was it actually seven o'clock? Growing up, she and Lydia had talked absolutely all the time, but as they got older, as Olivia embraced her role as a publisher and Lydia had become absorbed in her job at a prestigious law firm, they'd found it harder to connect for any conversation longer than a text message. They had decided to both set aside time at seven every Friday for a phone conversation so that they'd have a chance to reconnect and relax.

If it was seven, that meant Thomas had stayed until seven. Working on his database, probably, a searchable list of all their authors, their different works, approximate writing speed, preferred editors, target audiences, best contact information. She wasn't very demanding as a boss, generally. Her schedule was busy enough that she couldn't manage it on her own, but it wasn't intense enough to technically need 40 hours a week. But he'd been filling his extra time with organizing information throughout the company. He seemed to love it the way some people enjoyed putting together 1000 piece jigsaw puzzles upside down. It had only been a few days and she was already seeing the benefits in her day to day work life. When he put someone through to her office phone, he sent her a link in the new chat program that let her pull up all the information the company had on the specific author, letting her have effective, efficient conversations. It saved her time because she didn't need to try to find three different documents duplicated and spread over half a dozen different locations. It was consolidated, easy to reference, and it made her life easier. The little things he was doing, all of them made her life easier.

"Liv?"

She shook her head to refocus on her sister. "Sorry. It's been a long day."

Lydia took it in stride. "How's everything going?"

"Oh, you know." Sister code for "It kind of sucks, but what can you do?"

"Anything specific?"

Olivia leaned back in her chair and tried to figure out the right way to talk about any of it. As kids, they'd always spent more time talking about the men Lydia was interested in than anyone Olivia was dating; then Lydia had gotten married, and they'd mostly needed to avoid the topic of Lydia's lousy marriage. Olivia didn't have a lot of experience asking for advice for this stuff. Well, no time like the present to learn. "I hired this assistant."

Lydia's voice slipped easily into the high-pitched tones of their teenage years. "Oooo, tell me more! Is he handsome? Do you like him? Did you kiss him yet?"

Olivia took a long, deep breath, then forced the words out. "Yes, yes, and yes."

The pause on the other end of the line seemed endless. "Wait, what?"

"Okay, that's a lot of shocked tone for one little confession."

"Olivia. I have spent my entire life waiting for you to do something even mildly inappropriate so that I could lovingly tease my big sister, and now you do something worthy of a—well, they wouldn't make this movie for Hollywood, anymore, but definitely a movie for a streaming channel—and I'm supposed to be all 'oh my, how are you?'"

"Yes."

Lydia's voice dropped the mocking tone instantly. She must have heard the stress or worry in Olivia's tone. "Hey, big sister. How are you?"

It all spilled out very quickly after that. The problems with the business. The awkwardness of kissing her twenty-something employee. The hotness of kissing her twenty-something employee. There was a brief detour to scold Lydia for being disappointed that they hadn't, in her words, banged until the books fell off the bookshelves.

"So, you're trying to go cold turkey on the hottie assistant?"

"I'm trying not to flirt with him, at least. I'm trying to...just be work appropriate."

Lydia scoffed a little.

"What?" She wished she could see Lydia's face to understand whether her sister was teasing her or something else.

"If you wanted to behave yourself around the eye candy, you'd transfer him to a different department. One you went by every so often so you could enjoy the once-over, but not right outside your office as constant temptation. Why haven't you done that?"

Olivia ran her hand over her face and tried to think of a reason. "He's a really excellent assistant."

"How excellent?"

"He's been trying out different coffee blends all week to figure out which one I like best. I think he learned to make a pour over."

"Oh, he is fully into you." Lydia had the calm assurance of someone who was 100% capable of understanding other people's relationships far more than she was her own.

"He just wants to be good at his job."

"No. Being good at your job as an assistant means you memorize your boss's coffee order, not that you make them coffee yourself. You don't go and learn new types of coffee brewing methods for your boss." Another long pause. Olivia was pretty sure that she was supposed to say something, but she couldn't think of what. "Honey? Are you really okay?"

Her sister was always laughing, always silly, always making a joke. Hearing her be serious was a little concerning. "I...Lydia, I don't think I really am."

"What can I do?"

Olivia shrugged, trying to imagine her perfect world. What would be in it? "Tell me the magic spell that will save my business in the next three months."

A long sigh. "I promise that if I figure it out, you'll be the first person to know." Another pause that Olivia knew she should fill and couldn't. "And what are we going to do about your boy toy?"

"He's not—"

"Oh stop it. Look, do you like him?"

There was too much involved in that question. She didn't know all that much about Thomas, really. They'd been focused on work and—well, Olivia was pretty sure at this point that if she did ask him to bang her until the books fell down, he would happily oblige her. "I think I could like him."

"Then ask him out." Before Olivia could get a word out, Lydia continued. "Spare me the moral fortitude thing. So he's a little younger than you. So he's your employee. There's nothing illegal about it."

"There actually is—"

"No, it's illegal for you to harass him, it's not illegal for you to date him." Olivia could hear the lawyer brain kick in. "Although, you'd need to be careful in the actual workplace, because third parties have been able to successfully sue for sexual harassment."

"So make sure the office is empty before I bang him until the bookshelves come down?" She wasn't sure if Lydia didn't hear the sarcasm or didn't care. "Yeah, basically. I mean, you need to manage any jealousy from other employees to make sure they didn't feel like you were discriminating against them. Does your company have a policy about inter-office dating?"

"No."

"You really need to make one. Jesus, Olivia, have I taught you nothing?"

"Apparently not."

"But just don't...give him a special parking spot or whatever, and you'll be fine."

"I thought you wanted me to go on dates through some app. Meet a bunch of guys, you said."

Lydia scoffed. "What I want is for you to be happy. Will this guy make you happy? If so, I'm a big fan." Her voice softened. "Look, your whole romantic thing is weird to me. It seems like it is currently in the way of you getting what you seem to want. But I'm also not going to tell you what to do, you know? But you sound...different right now."

"Different?"

"Yes. You're obviously stressed about work and stressed about the company, and stressed about whatever else, but you talk about him...just go out on a date, if he wants to go."

It was the oddest feeling. Like some tiny flower spread open in her chest.

"Okay. I...I'll think about it. Okay."

Chapter 12

Thomas

The nice thing about getting caught up in your work and accidentally staying at your desk for almost two hours after everyone else left was that you definitely did not end up dealing with rush hour on the metro. He was also early enough to avoid the late-night-Friday crowd. Really, it was about the perfect time to be heading home.

He kept turning Olivia's question over in his head. What would make her app different from everyone else's? He could think of a million features, like voting, digital meet-and-greets, choose-your-own-adventure stories, that could all be used to distinguish an app. The problem was that he wasn't sure what features the Small and Sparkling readers would use. He was convinced that he could find an audience for the app, and was actually fairly sure that the simple branding would be enough to spread the audience. But Olivia clearly needed something more. Which was fair. "Build it and the audience will follow" was a strong ask for any company, but small ones in particular. She'd been right; building an app was expensive, and took time. Recruiting a new audience, teaching them a new ecosystem, training up a customer service staff. It was all investments. The way she'd talked about the project management software like the company was running scared for money, he wasn't sure that Small and Sparkling had a lot of spare capital to be throwing around.

If he was making a proposal for a client, he'd be doing market research right now, but if he was going to pull together something in a few days, he'd need an insider's perspective, and pretty close to immediately.

Well, his coffee expert was multipurpose. He texted his sister to find out when she was going to be putting her kids to bed so they could talk afterwards.

***

"So to clarify," Abby asked. "You're calling me to ask about bullet journaling, how to make coffee, and how to fix this woman's company for her just for funsies? And still insisting you're not into her."

Thomas rubbed his hand over his face, leaning on the kitchen counter. "Abby. You're making a very big deal about this one very specific point instead of answering the questions I'm asking you."

He could almost hear his little sister's shrug. "I am apparently your gateway to understanding this woman. I'm cool with being stubborn about it. So, tell me. What's going on?"

"She's not that into me, I think," he said. "She's very polite about it, but I think...I don't know. She's just not all that interested, apparently. So, what's the point in my being into her?""

"You are the least romantic human being alive. Possibly also the densest. Do you think it isn't romantic to learn about her favorite coffee and buy her journal supplies?"

No, based on everything he'd ever seen in every movie ever, it was roses and chocolate and standing outside windows with boomboxes that made up romance. This was just being a good person. "Please just answer my question."

Abby sighed the long-suffering sigh that could only come from being the youngest of four children. "So yes, to answer your mildly embarrassing question, I do have most of the romance serial novel apps downloaded, and I will not be telling you which ones I use the most. To respond to your really embarrassing question, you wretched programmer who sometimes forgets that people are people, not end users, I will not be telling you which ones I use the most or which heat levels I prefer, MY GOD THOMAS. You're ridiculous."

"Fine," he said. "I admit that was inappropriate." It had made sense as a question to ask, because how could he understand the best ways to incorporate the needs of the potential end user without understanding the target market? But then, maybe that thought was exactly Abby's point.

"Regarding your not creepy question, yes. I do really wish there were a couple of features that I saw more of. I wish I could follow authors. I wish I could leave comments on stories overall instead of just bit by bit. I wish I could get better notifications about new novels. God help me, I really do find 'if you like' recommendations and stuff like that helpful, as long as it's not too intrusive. Does that help?"

Thomas moved over to his desk, near the couch where Mason was playing some RPG on the console, and leaned over his computer. He typed a few notes and smiled. "It really does, Abby. Thank you so much." There was a pause as he tried to remember what to say next. Damn programmer-brain mode.

"Dad's not doing great," Abby said, introducing the most comfortable topic switch of all time. "The doctors are waiting to see if the new insulin can get things under better control, but right now, his sugars are really unstable, and they're worried." A long pause where he continued to not know what to say. "It would be nice if you were here to help. Ellie and Sharon and I are doing the best we can, but we all have lives and jobs, and Ellie's got the girls, and Sharon just got that promotion to district manager, and it's hard to juggle everything around the house since Mom passed anyway."

"I wouldn't be any help if I was there," Thomas said. "You're all very clear that I'm in the way and that I should just let everyone else take care of things." He tried to keep the bitterness out of his voice, but it didn't quite work.

The next sigh from Abby came from being the little sister who had the knack of keeping everyone organized and everything under control. Who desperately needed help she couldn't ask for, and that he didn't have the right skill set to offer anyway. If he could build an app that regulated a person's blood sugar and made sure their pancreas worked perfectly, he'd do it in a second. If he had the ability to edit his father's genetic code and remove the predisposition to alcohol dependence, he'd do that too. And if he could remove the memories of his own abusive childhood? No problem.

His father was, at his core, a very good person. He'd never been mean about his drinking, and it hadn't ever seemed excessive to anyone at home. But his pancreas had disagreed, and the resulting diabetes was turning out to be difficult to manage. He'd been twelve-stepping and rehabbing as hard as he could, but none of it was easy. For any of them.

"I'll do what I can," he said. "but I have to do it from here. Just...keep me updated."

"Yeah," Abby said, and he heard the silence of a dead line. Which was fair, all things considered. He texted her a thank you for helping with the research, she responded that she'd tell their parents that he sent his love, and they moved on. Until the next time they had to talk about it.

He swore, not politely, and tossed his phone at the couch cushion. It bounced in a deeply satisfying way before clattering to a stop safely next to the remote. Mason unpaused his game without a word, and Thomas started yet another bug check on his new code. Fifteen minutes later, he read the results of his latest build compile, swore even less politely, and started scrolling. After a minute, he sent the code to his laptop and dropped down onto the couch, where he could be miserable about his shitty build in peace. Mason chimed in from the other side of the couch, "Everything's going well then, I take it?"

Thomas spoke calmly, keeping his inflection steady and on complete lockdown. He chose the version of that question he wanted to answer. "I am ignoring you. I am ignoring you like I did the last twelve times you asked that question when this didn't work. Because if I don't ignore you, I'm going to find out how hard it is to code using a cracked monitor because I swear to God I missed a GOTO in here somewhere."

"That's one of the complicated ones, right?" Mason asked innocently, tapping on his phone to open an app and search up some menus. "Pepperoni or supreme?"

"Supreme, definitely, I want to pretend I'm eating a vegetable. Never code while feeling guilty." Thomas scanned the screen, using his non-mouse hand to point as Mason. "You minored in computer science, dude. We were in the same classes. You know this is the exact opposite of complicated." Thomas executed a quick macro, the equivalent of spellcheck but designed for code. Results: no errors. Perfect. That meant that whatever was going wrong was a major error, or worse, a complicated one. Because he was handling complicated problems so, so well right now. The nature of his complication flooded his thoughts, reminding him of the feel of her body, the warmth of her kiss, the need to pull her close...he growled a little as he adjusted himself and went back to typing. Dealing with his semi-hard cock was just par for the course after this week. Dammit.

Mason tapped his chin with his fingertip. Thomas managed not to roll his eyes. If he didn't know his friend, he'd consider the idea that Mason was about to say something incredibly sincere. "Huh, I guess I did go to those classes sometimes. That was where we met, I think. There was some crazy hard project I deal with once. Got totally stuck. Large or extra-large for the pizza?"

"Extra-large. What did you do?" Thomas shifted his attention to a section of the code that had absolutely been published at a point when he wasn't so much looking at his computer as trying to force it to power up with the energy generated by the sheer force of his glare.

Mason flashed a winning smile, the jerk. "I got so stuck that I had to get someone else's opinion on the whole thing. So, I called my buddy. He told me that if I walked away from the computer, I'd be able to clear my head and come to the problem with a fresh new perspective." He scrolled through the app a little more. "Cheese bread. One order or two?"

"Two. And I know exactly where you're going with this story, smartass, so don't even—"

Mason had absolutely no shame as he cut Thomas off, still grinning that smile that had gotten him through a thousand touchy situations with nervous investors. "And that buddy of mine? It was you!" His tone was the same as the end of a Scooby-Doo episode when the villain was finally unmasked.

Thomas looked up from his screen long enough to glare. "You, my friend, are a pioneer of comedy and pro-gramming. Your laugh-a-minute personality is how we turn those millions to billions. My coding isn't even a close second. We'll get you a standup special. Our target audience: anyone who took classes on how to write this stupid section of code but can't get it to work!" Thomas would have thrown something, but he'd run out of balled up socks, Hackey sacks, and the random pile of cat toys that Mason's ex-girlfriend had left under the coffee table. Unless he wanted to get up, collect every-thing, and bring them all back to his seat, there was no way to get them back. He'd have to find another way to channel his anger. "I'll figure this out. I can get this finished. I am not leaving here until I figure this out."

Mason, his best friend, his confidant, did the un-thinkable. He reached over and waved his hand in front of the screen. "Thomas. We need to talk about what's going on here."

Thomas looked at him, wildly unimpressed, slapping his friend's hand away from the very comforting logic that (at least in theory) was calculable and reliable. Once he got it working, it would keep working. He just had to get it working. "You know you're buying the pizza now, right?"

Mason's laughter was always infectious, and as he thew back his head and let loose, Thomas had to try not to smile. "Obviously, I offered. But seriously, you're actually losing your mind here over something that has no hard deadline and isn't even part of your job. I know that you've got this, and you'll figure it out eventually, but it would be helpful to know why your glare is causing things to combust before they burst into flame instead of after the conflagration."

Well, that got rid of the urge to smile. Bare his teeth, maybe, but yeah, grins were done for the moment. He stared at the ceiling and tried to breathe. "I'm having a day. This day has been a week, and the week has been a month. This girl, I do not know what to do with her."

"The boss, huh?" Mason finalized the order by waving his finger around with a little flourish before tapping on confirm. "What, did she flip out? Yell?"

"You know, if she'd done that, then at least I'd know what she was thinking." She'd stopped flirting out loud, but she hadn't stopped looking him up and down like he was edible. More discretely, more politely, more appropriate for the workplace. But not stopping.

"Ah, so that's what's going on." Mason jabbed Thomas in the ribs with his elbow. Thomas felt very charitable for continuing to pour his frustration into his code rather than the jabbing elbow and its owner. "What, you're nervous because she's your boss? You're a good dude, you've got nothing to worry about. Anybody who doesn't trust your best intentions has their head screwed on the wrong way."

Thomas typed for a solid minute before responding. He and Mason had fallen into this comfortable rhythm in school, and it was a foundational part of their friendship. It felt calming and settling, just like the code. "It's not that. It's a little that. Maybe a lot." He stared at the screen as he spoke, considering his options. "Which is better, a thread system in comments or just regular comments?"

"Comments. You have to avoid creating unmoderated mini-forums, especially with the number of minority creators that are writing."

Thomas sighed. "Right, forgot to account for people who weren't taught how to behave online. Why do we let the computer-illiterate on the internet again?" The look on Olivia's face as he'd walked toward her, slow and steady. When he'd asked her what she considered appropriate. In another setting, he would have asked her if she was behaving correctly. If she wanted him to show her how to behave. He considered how he would show her the ways she could relax, the ways she could give up control and let him make her feel good. How he could press her thighs apart as he kissed his way towards the sweetness between them. No. He shoved those thoughts away before sitting became actually uncomfortable. Focusing on how she'd left him alone, hard and without an explanation, did plenty to cool him down.

"If we kicked the computer illiterate off the internet, the entire economy would be destroyed, and our government would be unable to operate any system that was put in place to connect people in any kind of group." Mason was watching the app to ensure someone picked up their order.

"Oh, so the same as it is now, but with fewer annoying people on the internet." He decided to try a new approach on this stupid section. "Do we like endless scrollers? Or buttons to show more comments, like flipping a page?"

"Endless if you want reader engagement, page buttons if you have ads at the bottom," Mason said. "So, what, she's not into you?"

A memory of her going up onto her toes to kiss him flashed through his mind, followed by a thousand possibilities of where that memory could lead. "No. No, I don't think that's the case." He considered for a moment, then looked up from his screen to stare at the wall for a minute. "Okay, so if a woman kisses you—or you kiss her, and she's very clear that she's happy about that—then pushes you away and says she has to go, I don't know, wash her hair or something. What do you think is the general implication of all of that?"

Mason's phone gave a happy little chirp. He glanced at it and nodded. "Pizza will be here in twenty." He set it down on the couch. "She didn't look like she regretted it, did she?"

"No, she looked nervous. Like she didn't know what had happened."

"You kissed your boss, she freaked out, made an excuse and ran away." Mason leaned over Thomas's screen, looked over the visible code, and pointed. "Line 2037, close that function or you're going to be mad later."

Thomas hit the key and sighed. "Thank you. And yes. Yeah, I think freaked out is probably the best way to describe this. I freaked her out."

Mason hummed in thought. "You sure it's you and not her? Maybe she, I don't know, freaked out because she kissed her assistant and doesn't actually know if she's okay with that?" His attention turned on Thomas in a way that was distinctly unfamiliar in the context of their friendship. He could feel the focused totality of Mason's gaze and awareness, the sheer intensity that meant he could keep up with every asshole in the business world that Thomas had ever seen. "Okay. How far gone are you for her?"

Thomas waited a while to make sure he had all the words lined up and ready to go before he said anything. He tapped his fingers on the keyboard, too light to make any presses, but needing to keep his fingers moving. Everything was tense. He was working so hard to keep it under control, no matter how much he wanted to show her that he could do with his fingers. The careful movements that would make her shiver and the sharper ones that would make her scream. He wanted to hear both sounds, and all of the ones in between. He'd tried everything he could think of to manage how much he needed her, but nothing was making any kind of difference. "She makes it hard to know where I am. Makes me think of where I want to be." He started typing again, his fingers flying over the keys. "But she's scared. She's scared and running scared, maybe from me, maybe everything, but it's fear. I don't know how to fix fear. But I can fix this." He gestured at the screen, but he didn't say the rest of the sentence. It didn't need to be said. *Maybe that would be enough.*

The doorbell rang and Mason got up to grab the food from the door. He brought everything back to the couch along with a couple of paper plates and a roll of paper towels to manage the inevitable grease spills. "Okay. Rubber duck at finals rules are in effect. I'm turning on the console, and when we've gotten through this, I'll get us Chinese food that we won't have to warm up before eating when you stay up past dawn. Talk as much as you want, and I can pause the cutscenes in this game. You want to ask a question, I'll answer. Code or otherwise. Sound good?"

That familiar pattern was back in place. Thomas relaxed into it with an easy smile. "You got enough caffeine to keep me coherent while you try to get the good ending in your game this time?"

Mason passed him a bottle of fizzy and sugary along with a full plate of cheese bread and pizza. "Yeah. Just gotta take the right route this time, you know? See where I need to be, get there carefully. Put in the work."

Thomas nodded slowly. "Yeah. Put in the work." He took in a bite, and enjoyed the companionable silence as he started typing again. The soft clacking of the keyboard paired with the loud explosions of the game helped him take his mind off the problems in the code and actually see where they were. He started sorting out the contradictory instructions that were keeping him from getting a workable program. All he needed was a skeleton. Something good enough to impress a girl and show her the difference it could make for her business.

He'd eaten a couple slices of the pizza before he spoke again. "You have any idea why someone would be scared of me?"

"Scared of you, huh." Mason paused the game. "No reason at all. It's not always the dude causing the problem."

"Then what is she scared of?"

Mason took another bite of pizza and thought for a moment. He started the game back up again. "Could be a lot of things. But if it isn't someone on the outside, it's her. She's probably just scared of her. In whatever way that means for her."

Thomas couldn't keep the frustration out of his voice. "The fuck do I do then?"

Mason laughed. "Be safe and keep being a good guy. You're good at that. You think I moved you in here out of some weird noblesse oblige? I like you."

Thomas felt himself calm. "Thanks, man."

The conversation continued off and on until the sky started to light up. Mason said he needed to take a quick power-nap, and Thomas just nodded. He didn't quite remember when his friend came back, but when a fresh soda bottle turned up on the table, he muttered a quick thanks. The build was coming along better than it was last night.

Chapter 13

Olivia

It wasn't quite true that Lydia's suggestion, that she just ask Thomas on a date, had been rattling around in Olivia's head all weekend long. After all, there had been times she slept. Times she was sleeping and not dreaming of that soft, almost brusque laugh he had when she surprised him. The way he smiled when she made a suggestion or asked for something she thought would help her do her job more smoothly. He didn't say "as you wish," but if he had, she wouldn't have been surprised. Although she didn't get the sense he'd be the type to take orders for too long.

It was fair to say, however, that she had spent a good chunk of time considering what might happen if they did go out, and all of her thoughts were truly awful. What if one of them realized that their attraction was not actually reciprocated once they were in the same room together in a non-professional capacity? What were the odds, really, that this was true love, that they were both a moment away from being head over heels for each other? There was no question about their physical reactions to each other. But what about the rest of it? They knew so little about each other. For all of Lydia's reassurances, if they went out and they didn't have anything other than physical chemistry, and then later his performance as her assistant suffered, that terminating him would be harder. Riskier. She'd have to think about how to protect her company's reputation as well as her own heart. It seemed like so much to worry about. The thought of blind dates made her nauseated, but not as awful as losing...whatever it was that was being built here.

The preliminary weekend sales and readership reports were in her email. She'd avoided them all day, but she had to look at them before Monday was over. Her heart beat too fast as she opened them, even though she knew what they'd say. As she scanned the summaries and the raw data, she was tentatively happy to see that the numbers hadn't fallen further. One of their steady authors had started a new series, and a successful social media push seemed to have helped her readers follow to the new title. Social media impressions on the first chapters were promising. But their older works were staying at the same level, or starting to lose readers over time.

She knew it made sense. People always fell out of a series over time. More people read book one than book two, and book two than book three, and so on. After a given point, going back to the beginning to read forward was a daunting task and it killed the desire to read the series at all.

"Everything alright?" Thomas was standing in her office door, holding a mug of coffee. He lifted it slightly. "It's late, and I know you've been busy today. Need a pick-me-up?" She couldn't help smiling, and he stepped into the office.

She had been busy; she hadn't had a chance to actually talk to him in the morning as he went over her schedule. Throughout the day, she'd been firing questions at him and getting quick answers, but she hadn't even had a chance to really say hello. She didn't need to ask him out, but she'd like to at least be personable. "Fine, just going over some figures from the weekend. Anything interesting happen for you over the last few days?"

He sat down across from her, handing her the coffee and pulling out his tablet and what she knew would be today's sticker list for her bullet journal. "Busy week-end. Got an idea for something and spent most of the weekend with my head in it." One of those short laughs she was coming to love so much. "It was a little bit of a coding marathon, really. My roommate finally made me go to bed early this morning. I was worried I would accidentally oversleep, but after I laid down, he set four alarms at slightly different times and at various different locations in the room, so there wasn't a chance of that."

His eyes were a bit bloodshot, and there was that slight puffiness around the eyes that she associated with her own all-night work sessions. "Did you enjoy it?"

His head tilted just a little and she was rewarded with a tiny smile that was one of the most real things she saw in her day. "I did, actually. I have to say, most people don't hear about a 48-hour straight coding session and sincerely ask if the person enjoyed it."

She tried to keep her voice level. "If your work is enjoyable and you get excited enough doing it that your body blocks out everything but the work—obviously it's not a sustainable practice over the long term, and I always say that crunch is a failure on the part of management, but when the creativity is there and you get the chance to just flow with it, it must be fantastic."

That small smile got bigger. "You think coding is creative?"

Now she was just a little nervous. "I mean, don't you? You're taking a string of letters and words—many of them do not make sense, I'll note—and put them in a specific order, and when you're done, you get this beautiful piece of the world that is more than the sum of its parts. If that's not creative, then I'm not sure what is."

He was staring at her now in a way she didn't know how to interpret. "I've...never met anyone who wasn't a programmer who thought like that."

She shrugged, still nervous. "I don't know anything beyond some really basic CSS, just enough to have gotten me in trouble five years ago and probably wildly out of date now, but seeing how just a small change to the words behind the website affected the way the words on the website shifted and changed, it was incredible. Do you know one of the most important pieces of advice we give to authors who are struggling to understand how their books will flow as a whole?"

"No, please tell me."

"We have a preview option where they can plug in their text and see what the story is going to look like on the site itself. Most people tend to put that up and then just scroll through really quickly to make sure that there aren't random image anchors showing up in weird places or something, but we really encourage them to make edits there. It's easy to see when you have incredibly long paragraphs, or too many short ones in a row, and I tell you, there's no better spellcheck than seeing something published online. You immediately see every misplaced comma and 'teh' that ever existed. The trick was making sure they couldn't accidentally publish the document from that preview. It only happened a few times, but the trouble it caused was more than enough." It occurred to her that Thomas probably would have planned for that and organized everything correctly from the start.

If only she'd had someone like him with her when everything started. He would have been able to build everything up correctly. As he'd worked to improve her ability to access everything over the last week, she'd been shocked at how many redundancies he'd eliminated that she hadn't even seen were there. She didn't have less work to do, but she wasn't doing the same thing twice. And, delightfully, he didn't seem to be on the verge of making any people redundant. Just unifying their information so that she could see everything at once.

He nodded. "So how are the weekend numbers looking?"

"Pretty good, actually." She gestured to him to come around the desk. He hesitated for a moment before moving, and she blushed. The last time he'd come around to her side of the desk, things had absolutely gotten interesting. Clamping down on her feelings, she pointed to a few different numbers. "I was worried because I knew this author was going to be picking up a new series this week. She had a pretty good social media push, so most of her audience followed her to her new story. That's not a given, especially if they don't see the messages the authors put out, or they aren't as active on social media. So, this is a good sign. She didn't change subgenres or tropes this time, so I'm confident that a lot of them will stick around."

"Readers don't get notifications when favorite authors have new stories out?"

She shook her head. "They get emails when a new chapter of a story they favorited comes out, but not a new story by an author they liked previously. When we started this, I focused on how people would like a given story, and by the time we all figured out that they might want to just read the next thing that someone wrote, it was too late to build in the functionality. Or so I was told. At that point, the website and UI were far beyond what I was able to edit or manage on my own."

She looked at Thomas, leaning past her with his hands on her desk, studying the figures. She was suddenly hyperaware of herself. The knee length black skirt she'd worn this morning because she loved how it hugged her hips. The dark blue sleeveless shell with the tiny little buttons that made her feel delicate. She hadn't planned for him being this close when she'd grabbed her undergarments, though. She'd worn a matching set just for the luxury of it, and the bra was very light. No extra padding to hide how her nipples were reacting to the heat gathering through her body. In fact, the silky fabric of her top made them stand out.

His torso was roughly over her lap. If she moved forward to kiss his cheek or his neck, her breasts would press into his arm. It would be a simple movement for him to shift his weight from the desk to the arms of her chair, and from there, she wasn't sure what would happen. The tightening in her body told her that she would almost certainly like it. But kissing him like that wouldn't be asking him on a date. Or, it might be, but it wasn't the sort of date that started with dinner and a movie.

Of course, dinner could happen in bed. Small bits of fruit and cheese and whatever fed to each other. Kissing fingers clean. Slow undressing, soft kisses and caresses leading to something more. Leading to something sweaty and groaning and hard that was still, somehow, as romantic as the night began it. After all, hadn't that always been the point? That sex could be amazing, hot, wonderful, and still be fueled by romance? Fitzwilliam Darcy would never be caught in bed like that, but what if Jane Austen had been able to write a bit more freely about the sexual parts of her romances? After all, there was the old saying about a gentleman in the streets and a beast between the sheets. She'd always thought of Darcy as the ultimate gentleman, awkward as hell but entirely aware of the way the world saw him and the way he must preserve his good name. The way he'd done right by the Bennets at the end. The way he'd taken care of Lizzy when she needed it the most. Someone bringing her coffee and taking such care to make sure that her office was set up to please her specifically. The sweet, constant politeness. That could absolutely be considered gentlemanly.

Thomas had turned his head and was looking at her now, the smile on his face still soft, but much hungrier. Still touching politeness, still not overt, still almost sweet, but wanting. If he'd noticed the physical signs of her desire, he wasn't going to draw attention to them. "Something on your mind?"

One of his hands shifted to rest ever so lightly on the arm of her chair. An offering. Not an invitation, not anything more than that. Just a little touch of reminding her that there was more, if she wanted to take it.

"No, no," she managed to squeak out. "I was just admiring your...shoulders. Do you work out?"

Oh for the love of everything. Had those actual words just come out of her mouth? Was she that meek? How completely ridiculous.

He stood up, resting his ass on her desk and braced himself with his hands. She had to move her chair back a little to make room for him without her face being at, well, right at a tempting level. She was struck again by how solidly built he was, and she absolutely forbade herself from looking down to see if he was as turned on as she was. "I lift some," he said. "Nothing dramatic, but I like to avoid the stereotypical programmer noodle arms and hunched neck. People just tend not to notice because I, you know, eat bread and don't intentionally dehydrate myself to a dangerous level just to look like a superhero."

The echo of her own thoughts made her shiver. Her brain—or something much lower—sent her an image of how he could use all that muscle to hold her at just the right height to drive into her while her back was pressed against a wall, lifting her leg high around his waist so that he could go as deep as he wanted.

She tried to shake the thoughts loose from her mind without actually shaking her head in the world's most obvious gesture. She smiled, shooting for pleasant conversation instead of an urge to run her hands up his cotton poplin shirt and feel all that tempting strength. Ask him what he might be able to do with it.

Ask him on a date, Lydia's voice whispered to her. *Do it, or you'll regret it forever.*

"Aren't we ridiculous?" She tried for a lightweight, laughing tone, but ended up with something breathy that made his pupils dilate and his throat work. "The boss and her assistant. The older woman and the younger man. How many tropes do we fall under?"

His voice had dropped lower. She got the sense that he had an iron grip on his control right now. "Office romance. Slice of life?" He grinned, but it wasn't that soft and sweet smile she'd gotten used to. This one shot straight to her thighs and made them tighten. "Is that something you fantasize about?"

Yes. At least lately. She tried to say no, but only came out with more squeaky mouse sounds.

"I'm sorry," he said, but she didn't think he sounded sorry at all. "I didn't mean to make you uncomfortable." That one she believed. "But the only way we're ridiculous or a trope is if we're setting up for a hot romance." That grin again. "Or are we doing a will-they-won't-they? A little bit of Sam and Diane to keep the audience tuning in?"

"Do you want to go out with me?"

Based on the look on Thomas's face, she wasn't sure which of them was more shocked.

Chapter 14

Thomas

Close your mouth, you idiot, before you catch a fly. Thomas was fairly sure he looked like a shocked anime character, complete with stress lines in the background and a wide, rectangle mouth. This was the goal of all this flirting, wasn't it? Getting her attention, convincing her that he was interesting as a partner, that he was worth going out with?

His hand was still resting on the arm of her chair, and he didn't know what to do about that. If he leaned forward and kissed her—wouldn't that be too on the nose? Relatively speaking. If he pulled back, though, that would be awkward. She might think he was saying no.

And then, like she had the first time they kissed, she reached up, slipped her hand around the back of his neck, and pulled him down to her mouth. There was no gentle exploration this time, though. He claimed her mouth as soon as she touched him, letting the low, hungry sounds he'd been keeping to himself for days rumble through his chest. She made a little whimpering sound that went straight to his cock and had him rock solid before he could blink. He wrapped his hands around her waist and pulled her up to him, leaning back ever so slightly on the desk so that her weight fell onto him. He curved her hand around her ass and pulled her tight so that there was no question about whether she'd feel him hard against her. He was only a little taller than her, so he pressed into the lowest part of her belly. If he stripped away their clothing, lifted her up at all, he could be inside of her. She trembled like she knew it. "Thomas..." she murmured against his mouth.

"Tell me to stop if you want me to stop." His voice was rough and taut. He tried to be gentle with his words, but there was something fierce inside him, something he rarely let show, and he was not in a mood to be gentle.

"The door's still open..."

He pulled back just enough that he could see her face, take her in. She looked a little nervous, the corner of lip between her teeth. But he could also see her nipples, tight and hard against her tank top. She hadn't worn one of those thick, molded bras today, apparently. She'd either been confident in her ability to hide any attraction she was feeling or she hadn't cared.

I have to let her choose. She has to choose this. I can't keep doing this if she isn't choosing it.

"Either close the door or tell me to leave. One or the other, Olivia. Pick."

She gasped at the harsh tone in his voice, but given the way she pressed herself against him, she wasn't complaining about it. She didn't move.

"I mean it," he said. It was agony not to be kissing her, to be stroking her, to be inside her. "I need you to pick. It's your call, your choice, your decision. I will do what you want me to do. But I am not going to press anything on you. I am not going to do anything you don't want me to do. So, you need to pick."

He wanted to trace his hand down her side, rub a circle over her nipple with his thumb, pull her against his cock again, let his body make a promise to hers. But this had to go at her pace. Even if it killed him.

"Okay," she said, her voice was quiet and steady. Calm. A professional tone he knew too damn well. He took a deep breath and prepared himself for yet another rejection. She stepped back from him and moved around the desk. Away from him. To the door. He stood, ready to be told to go, this time not to come back. She'd asked him out, sure, kissed him, sure, but not this. This was too much, and she'd scared herself again, and he had to be okay with that, he had to stopped pushing.

He was so wrapped up in her thoughts that he almost didn't hear the click of the door shutting. The sound of the lock flipping, though, that got his attention.

"It's after four," she said, her voice conversational. "If anyone comes by, they'll assume that I've just left early for the day and gave you the afternoon off." And then she was quiet, watching him. Waiting, he realized. She'd picked. Now it was up to him to lead.

"Come here," he said. He sat down in her chair, deeply pleased that she preferred the kind of office chair where the arms flipped up. She did as he said, but there was nothing meek about it. He liked that. With the arms of the chair out of the way, he could tug her forward until she had to spread her legs wide to accommodate his thighs between hers. She barely had enough room to stand, which was fine with him. If she sat down, she'd be in his lap. "I need you to understand something. Okay?"

She nodded.

"You picked. But you need to understand that you can change your mind. I want you more than I think you can imagine, but saying yes once doesn't mean you can't say no if something feels uncomfortable. Okay?"

She nodded again.

"I need to hear you say it. For me to be okay, I need to hear it."

She swallowed twice and then said, clear and loud, "Yes."

His cock twitched, hard. "Thank you." He ran his hands up her outer thighs to cup her full ass in his hands. "Now. Tell me if this skirt can go up to your hips without ripping."

She thought for a moment. "Yeah. It should be fine."

"Oh, very good." He tightened his hands on her again and she made a little moan. "Quiet, now. You don't want anyone to hear us. Remember, we left early. No need for them to check and see what's going on."

"Sorry," she murmured, her eyes half closed. Oh, he was going to enjoy every second of this.

"Pull that skirt up for me. Nice and slow." He tried to keep the growl in his voice under control, but the way she was shivering at every word was making it hard. She teased the skirt up nice and slow, just like he wanted. He followed the hem with his thumbs, tracing up the soft skin of her inner thighs until the hem of her skirt was just barely covering her. "Are you feeling shy, Olivia?"

She was biting the corner of her lip again, but her eyes were wide open, and all of her attention was focused on him. "Yes."

"Can you tell me why?" A gentle voice now, soft and encouraging. Open. Keep all that hunger to himself for the moment, no matter how much it hurt to keep it chained. There would be time to let loose later. Maybe not this afternoon, though. He needed to focus on her for now.

"What if you don't like what you see?"

Her voice was soft and kittenish, and it took everything he had not to laugh. He took her ass in his hands again and pulled her forward so he could kiss her covered belly. "Since the first time I saw you, all I could think about was how beautiful you are. How soft your curves looked. How it would feel to be able to press my fingers into you, grip you, hold you. Press against you. I love how you look." He kissed her stomach again, then leaned back and looked up at her face. Her eyes were so wide. "Will you show yourself to me?"

She took a deep breath and tugged her skirt up those last few inches. It was bunched entirely around her waist now, and her panties were on display. Pretty blue lace with a delicate little bow. God, was there nothing about her that wasn't perfect and adorable? She kept her hair trimmed rather than waxed, which he loved. People should do what they wanted with their own body hair, but this was his favorite look. Tamed, but not bare.

Her hands were shaking. He leaned forward again and pressed a kiss against her mound, and then against the swell of her lower belly. She made a happy sounding little exhalation and pressed into his mouth. He wondered if she even knew she was doing it.

"You're so beautiful," he said, kissing her again. "You're absolutely gorgeous." He traced his thumbs up her thighs with enough pressure to avoid tickling her and traced the hems of her panties. "There are so many things I could do to you right now. So many ways to enjoy you, to make sure you enjoy yourself. This is all about you, Olivia. I'm entirely focused on you. Nothing else matters but you right now. Do you understand?"

She looked skeptical as she nodded. Well, then. He slid his right thumb under the hem of her panties. She was spread wide enough as she stood over him that he could press inside her labia and find her clit. He didn't do much except apply pressure, firm and direct, but she gasped hard. She shook, and one hand went to the back of the chair to balance herself, but she didn't let go of her skirt.

And then, the motherfucking phone rang.

They both jumped, the shared moment shattering around them. Olivia stepped back, blinking rapidly. She shook her skirt back down over her hips. She reached for the phone, then paused and pressed another kiss to his lips. He kissed her back, but a bit more reserved now. Cautious. "I'm not panicking," she said. "I'm not running away. I'm going to take this call. We can both take a minute to breathe. And then I want to...to go somewhere where we can talk. Have a meal. I want to make sure that I want this with all of me, not just the part of me that you make all hot and bothered. You...deserve all of me. So this is just a pause, okay? Not a stop."

His heart was pounding with relief and happiness and need, all at once. "That sounds good to me."

"Awesome." She picked up the phone, said hello, and then sat directly down in his lap. She was sitting sideways, so her hip was up against his cock. He'd been softening, but when she reached to wrap his arm around her waist and then put her head on his shoulder, he was sure she could feel him hard against her. She gave a small wiggle, pressed herself closer to him, and kissed his neck before saying into the receiver, "This is Olivia Michaelson. How can I help you?"

He smothered the sounds he wanted to make as she shifted on his lap again. Oh, two could absolutely play this game. He pressed his fingers into her thighs again, hard enough to make her lift her head and give him wide, innocent eyes. He raised his eyebrows and started pressing his thumbs up again. She was sitting on her skirt, so there was no way to press it up as high as it had been, but he could get his thumbs tantalizingly close, enough that she had to bite her lip to stay quiet.

The voice on the other end of the phone was so loud that he couldn't help but overhear. "Olivia! Hello! I've been trying to get ahold of you for a long time now, but I couldn't get past your assistant. Hell of a girl, but she's got a pretty tight grip on you, doesn't she?"

Olivia leaned back to look at Thomas. He shook his head, putting his free hand up in the air to indicate he had no idea what this guy on the phone was talking about. "I'm sorry we haven't been able to connect. And, sorry, but who am I talking to?"

Thomas wrapped his arms around her again and started teasing the little buttons on her top. To his delight, they were real buttons. He started flicking them open one by one, watching Olivia as he did it. She mouthed "no" at him, but her mouth was open in silent laughter. "Yes," he whispered. She put her hand over the mouthpiece and put a finger over his lips to shush him. Oh, on another day, she'd pay for that in a way that both of them would love.

"What was that?" The man on the phone asked.

"Oh, nothing, sorry," Olivia said. "I was trying to flag down my assistant to ask her why in the world she wasn't letting what is clearly the most important call of

my day get through to me." Thomas could hear the sarcasm thick in her voice, but the phone man didn't seem
to get it. "And, sorry, who is this?"

He'd flicked open enough buttons to slip his hand
into her top and squeeze her heavy breast. She made
a sound that she managed to transform into a breathy
little laugh. The man laughed along with her. "This is
Evan Lowry. Wow, she really didn't tell you anything,
did she?"

Thomas rolled her nipple between his thumb and
forefinger and Olivia's eyes flew wide before they shut
hard. She shifted on his lap, which hiked her skirt up
a little higher. She tried to stand and shuffle it down
again, but he held her in place. "I guess she didn't!" She
hid the little gasp in her voice with the rise at the end
of the word. She tried another playful glare and tried to
turn away from him. That was a strategic error on her
part. He let her turn until her back was to his front and
then pinned her in place against him. Just holding her,
letting her feel his painfully hard cock against the small
of her back. Then rolling his hips against her. "So, what
can I do for you?"

"Olivia, Liv. Do you mind if I call you that?"

"I really do, actually. I'm starting to understand why
my assistant didn't put your call through, Mr. Lowry."
Emphasis on the title. "I'm very busy." Her skirt had
hiked up far enough that he could press his fingers into
her panties again. Not with any real movement, not like
he had at first, but enough that she could feel him.

She rocked against him, hard, and he wrapped his arm around her hips, holding her in place while he ground his cock into her. She had the mouthpiece tilted up and away from her mouth now because her breath was unsteady. His free hand went back to her nipple, taunting her. She tried to turn and glare, but he just whispered in her ear. "You started this. Do you want me to stop?"

She arched into him again. He took that as a no.

"I'm a producer," Lowry said, some of the smarm gone from his voice now. "TV and movies, but mostly TV. Prestige drama, limited series, the stuff you see on streaming networks and tell all your friends about. I think you and I could do incredible work together."

Olivia put her hand firmly over Thomas's, and he stopped moving. She sat up slowly. "I'm sorry. What are you talking about?"

"The TV rights to your novels. I want to know who has them, and I want to know who to talk to about getting them. I think they're amazing stories, and I think they could make incredible visuals."

She spun the chair so that she was facing her computer, still sitting on Thomas's lap. He kept his hands on her hips to hold her steady and tried to give her a little space so that his cock would not be as distracting to her as it was to him. Lowry kept up a steady stream of meaningless patter as Olivia made small "I'm listening" noises and ran a quick web search on his name. Thomas knew it already, and so when Olivia's screen filled with bad CGI monsters and doggie style sex so that the tits were swaying, he was prepared for her to bristle with rage. He dug his fingers into her hips a little to keep her balanced emotionally. She might not ever want to work with Evan Lowry, but pissing him off wasn't going to do the business any favors.

"Thanks so much for your call, Mr. Lowry," she cut in, using a tone that was very professional and sharp enough to slice granite. "But I don't think there's going to be a good fit between your projects and mine. I hope you do well in your future endeavors." Lowry was still speaking when she hung up the phone. She tried to spin around, but Thomas held her in place on his lap; all she managed to do was spin the chair. "You made that hard on purpose!" She was laughing as she fell back, her head on his shoulder again.

"You made the choice to sit on my lap to take your phone call," he said. "I figured you knew what you were getting yourself into."

"Oh, is that so?"

"It is." God, this woman was incredible. Responsive to his touch and his playfulness. And the side of him that was just a little bit darker. That really enjoyed telling her what to do and seeing her do it. "Still want to go out to dinner with me?" He tried to his tone level and playful, but there was a need there that caught him off guard.

If she noticed it, it didn't faze her. "More than ever."

Chapter 15

Olivia

Ten minutes into dinner, and Olivia desperately wished that they'd finished what they'd started in the office before leaving. She knew she'd made the right call by pausing what they were doing. Thomas was a good man, and he deserved more than just being her stress relief. She liked him, and she wanted him, but she needed to know that both were there. And that he liked her, too. That...maybe this could be more than just good sex. Or at least, if it wasn't going to be anything but good sex, they both needed to know that. Agree on that. Hell, she was thirty now, maybe it was time to give casual sex a try.

She'd left it to Thomas to choose, and he'd opted for an Indian place a few blocks away. If he knew it was close to her place, he didn't give any sign of it. It was a family style restaurant, and since he was familiar with their menu, she told him she wanted saag paneer and then let him pick the rest of the dishes.

"So, you know plenty about me," she said, after biting into the first perfect samosa. It was the only way in the world she was willing to eat peas. "Tell me a little about yourself. I know you love the creative side of programming and minored in English. What else?"

"Let's see. I'm the youngest kid of four, and the only boy. My parents live in New England, in a pretty rural spot. My grandparents were dairy farmers, but my father was—is—a math professor at a nearby university. They still live on the farm, but it hasn't been working land in a long time. My sisters are all scattered around the area, but a lot closer than I am. My mom passed a few years ago." There was something he wasn't sharing in there, but she didn't want to push. "What's your favorite book—" he cut her off before she could speak. "That isn't by Jane Austen."

She thought of mentioning *A Room with a View*, but she wasn't sure he'd get the joke. "I like a lot of modern speculative fiction, actually. Books that ask 'what-if' are always intriguing. Even if I don't agree with the answer, I like to see what happens when the question is asked."

"And romance is 'what if love is real?'"

"More, 'what if I get to be loved?' In a really good romance, the reader can see some aspects of themselves reflected. That's why I think it's so important to make sure that as many people can publish romance novels as possible. So everyone can see themselves as worthy of love." He was studying her so hard that she considered tossing a piece of naan at him to distract him. "What?"

"You're just fascinating. That's all."

The words "am not" popped up, but she avoided saying them. She also discarded the equally useless "no, you are." She eventually managed, "Thank you."

"You're welcome. Do you like sports?"

She shrugged. "I'll watch them if they're on, and I know enough about the rules to know which side I'm cheering for. I don't follow any teams. What about you?"

"Nah. My sisters were all superstars at one sport or another and I had to go to all of their games. My hand eye coordination sucks and I only like being sweaty in very specific circumstances." He gave her an absolutely lecherous grin. "I'm very stereotypical in this way. What superpower would you want?"

She was pretty sure he was doing the rapid fire questions on purpose to try and catch her off guard. The problem was that he wasn't asking hard questions. "I need two."

"You can't."

"Then I don't want any."

He rolled his eyes. "Fine. What two? But you have to tell me what you'd want to do with them. To explain why you need both."

"I want to fly in any atmosphere, and I want to be invulnerable. I want to fly to Jupiter and see what's inside the red spot." She took a bite of chicken tikka while he stared at her. "You were expecting something boring, weren't you?"

"Where have you been all my life?" He stared at her like she'd hung the moon, and she didn't think he was faking it at all.

Waiting for Mr. Darcy. "You know, here and there. I've lived in this city for most of it. Grew up here, went to college here, work here now. I love it here. What about you?" There was absolutely no way she was engaging with his starry eyes. Not right now. They were twisting something up inside of her, and she didn't dare to hope for what he seemed to be offering. They'd known each other for two fucking weeks. She'd told Lydia a million times: love at first sight wasn't real. Lust at first sight, sure. But it was romance, caring for a person, loving them, treating them well, showing them your heart bit by bit, that was what built the kind of love that could last when things got hard. She couldn't believe in love. Not yet. Romance, sure. He was wooing her with his coffee and his office supplies and his making sure that he was always there when she needed something, even if it was just a reminder that starting to yell at some Hollywood producer was a bad idea. Maybe it wasn't traditional, flowers and chocolates, but if romance was about feeling cared for, he was pulling that shit off like crazy.

"Are you asking if I like the city?" She nodded. "It's definitely growing on me." He let his eyes slide down to her breasts and the top she hadn't quite buttoned all the way back up, then lifted his gaze to hers again. She placed her hand over her chest in mock irritation, and he laughed. "Beyond that? I don't know. This is the place where I can do what I want to do, but it's different than where I grew up, and different than where I went to school. Everything's faster, bigger, more."

"A lot of tech work is remote, though, these days."

"And a lot of it is hybrid. And with all the companies laying people off, you have to be able to be flexible. Being here means that I can find more opportunities than I can working off the shitty wi-fi in a tiny town."

"Even if you're far from your family?"

He shrugged, and she got that same sense that there was something he was keeping to himself. "We're not all that close. We don't fight, exactly. I'll go home for holidays. But we get along better with me out here." A long silence that she didn't know how to fill. "And what about you? Family?"

"A younger sister. Lydia. Our grandparents passed several years ago; that's actually where I got the seed capital to start Small and Sparkling."

"Parents?"

"Both of them are still alive. They're...special. Our dad's a little distant, our mom's a little wildly overinvolved, and when we were younger, she was kind of obsessed with marrying us off. I think it's part of why Lydia married so young."

Olivia was quiet, waiting for the next question, but it didn't come. Something had shifted in the conversation, and she wasn't quite sure how to wake it up again.

It took about ten minutes of fairly light commentary on the food and the day to day life in the office before he really spoke again. "Look, I really suck at small talk. I'm sorry. It's just not in my skill set. On my list of to-dos is to program a neural net that can do all the small talk for me."

She asked him how that would work, and their conversation was vibrant for the rest of the meal. And then, as they had the leftovers boxed up, Olivia only hesitated a moment before asking him to come home with her.

The rideshare to her house was agonizing. He pulled her as tight against him as he could without actually pulling her into his lap, and his hands were dancing over every part of socially acceptable bit of skin they could find. Trailing down her neck, running up her thighs, stroking the back of her hands. She wanted nothing more than his mouth on hers, and every second that she wasn't kissing him was a crime.

She'd spent dinner trying to untangle it all. Did she want him for himself, or for how he made her feel? Was this just going to be sex, or was there the possibility for something more? She didn't know, and she had no idea how to figure it out. Outside her door, she paused, her hand on his chest. "I have absolutely no idea what I'm doing," she said. Honesty was the best policy and all of that, but she really hoped she wasn't fucking this up beyond all imagination. "I know I want you, but I have no idea what comes after…" she gestured at the door, trying to imply everything that lay beyond the threshold, the night, the morning, the rest of her life.

He kissed her, searing hot. He tasted like curry and cinnamon. "I want this. I want you. I'm okay with letting whatever happens next just happen." He pulled back and studied her. "Are you okay with that?"

Honesty. Honesty. "I don't know. But I don't know what else to do but try."

He smiled, and her heart melted. "I can live with that."

Inside, she expected him to press her back against the door and ravish her there, carry her off to the bedroom and toss her down on the bed before taking what was his. Or something like that. Instead, once the door was closed behind them, he threaded his fingers through hers. "Want to give me a tour?"

She managed not to laugh out of sheer nervousness. "Sure." She led him to the kitchen, showed him all the different coffee pots and blends and answered all the questions he asked. She showed him the living room and her small office. Then she took him to the bedroom. He ran his hands over the soft purple duvet cover and then reached for her. She went to him easily, kissing him, feeling the urgency building between them. And then he pulled away just a little, lifting both of her hands to his lips, one at a time.

"I said before that there were so many ways to enjoy you, Olivia, and I meant it." He kissed the insides of her wrists, then moved to press his lips against her neck, just below her ear. She let out a shivery little gasp. Everything had been so firm in the office, so passionately heated.

This was different. This was a calmer version of Thomas. No, not calmer. Banked. The fire held in control. "I have so many thoughts. What I can do to you. How I can enjoy you. I promised you my full and complete attention earlier, and I still want to give you that. How does that sound to you?"

His lips pressed into her throat, tilting her head back, and she used those broad shoulders to keep her balance. His hands came to her waist, tightening there. "Yes," she said. "Yes, I think that sounds very good."

He made a happy sort of humming sound. "And do you have any ideas about what you might like? What might make you feel very good?" His fingers crept down her body, splaying over her ass, pulling her tight against him—and he was very hard again, incredibly hard—and then sliding to the front of her skirt, cupping her mound through the fabric that suddenly seemed both too thick and too thin.

"I don't know," she said, trying to keep her voice from sounding too thin and reedy. Her mind was pulled in a million directions and she couldn't articulate an idea, much less choose one.

"I see," he said, his voice dropping and his hands sliding up her body this time, teasing over those tiny buttons on her blouse without opening them. "Then maybe it's time for me to make some decisions. Would you like that?"

That sounded calming. Relaxing. She spent so fucking much time making decisions. Letting him take care of that for a little bit. That would be gorgeous. Her panties were soaking wet, her mind was racing, and she knew she wanted him. He could take care of the details. "I'd like that," she said. "I'd like that a lot."

He smiled at her like he was proud of her. "Thank you," he said. "God, you're so incredibly beautiful." His thumb brushed over her taut nipple and she arched against him, pressing into his hand. He laughed quietly. "I noticed that you liked that before. When you were talking on the phone. When you started teasing me."

She thought about arguing that she hadn't, that she'd only meant to make sure he didn't think she was walking away or turning him down, but she was absolutely the one who'd started wiggling her ass on his lap. "I don't usually," she said. "This is all you."

"You know," he said, one hand cupping her breast and spinning idle circles around her nipple while the other kneaded her ass and kept him pressed hard against him. "We were interrupted earlier. I had plans all thought out that we didn't get to enjoy. What do you think about resuming where we left off?"

Where she'd had her skirt around her waist, and he'd been thumbing her clit and about to do who knew what while she promised not to make a sound. "Yes."

"Good. Thank you. But you have to promise me something, okay? If I'm making the choices, you have to promise that you'll tell me if something doesn't feel good. It only works if you're enjoying what's happening. Understand?"

She nodded and he flicked her nipple hard enough that it stung.

"I need you to say it. That you promise."

Her head was full of lust and wool. "I promise. If I'm not enjoying something, if it doesn't feel good, then I'll tell you."

He kissed her, and all that banked heat was suddenly bursting forth, tearing through her and leaving her gasping. She pulled him as close as she could, desperate to touch him. He kissed her back for a moment, then stepped away, taking her hand in his. "Show me that office again."

She led him through the house to the small office off the living room. She didn't use it that often; she usually collapsed with her laptop on the couch or worked on her tablet at the kitchen table. Inside the office, he turned in a slow circle. "Does the door lock?"

"Yes."

"Good. Lock it. Just like before."

Her body clenched. In the office, when she'd had to be quiet, because even though it was the end of the day and it was unlikely someone would come looking for them, it wasn't impossible. And she couldn't risk being found out. Fucking someone in her office like that. Humiliating. She turned and locked the door behind them. When she turned back, he was sitting in her desk chair again, his erection tenting his pants like he was made of marble.

"Now come here, beautiful," he said. "Get your skirt up."

She didn't hesitate this time, just tugged it up to her waist, exposing her panties to him. He splayed his hand over them then dipped down, pressing the pad of his thumb into her clit. He nudged her thighs open with his knees, making another of those little humming sounds. "Yes. Almost here. But...wait, no." He pressed her knees open further and then dipped his fingers under the hem of her underwear, giving one long stroke from her clit down to her opening and back. She gasped, catching herself before she fell, her hand balancing on the back of the chair.

"Yes. Yes, that's exactly where we were." He leaned forward and pressed a delicate kiss to her belly. "And I remember just what I was going to ask you. I was going to ask if you liked these panties." He tugged at the elastic around her legs.

"I do."

"Then get them off before I shred them." His voice was hard again, demanding, and it shot through her like a blade. "Skirt too."

She unzipped her skirt and shimmied out of it and the panties, then stood there, half nude and waiting. The air felt chilled, but whether it was because of her heated skin or because it was actually cold, he didn't know. He left her standing there for a moment, studying her.

"From here, I have to admit, I had a few different thoughts. I thought about pulling you into my lap and having you rock on my hand until you came. The big problem was that if I didn't take off my pants, I was fairly sure you'd leave a big wet mark on my lap. And if I took off my pants and had you in my lap, I didn't think I'd be able to keep my focus on you." He reached out and took her hands, pulling him toward her until she was straddling his thighs. If he pulled her down, she'd be sitting in his lap, her cunt slotted up neatly against his cock, and she absolutely would leave a soaking wet spot on him. No question. "So, I think I'm going to go with plan A." He stood up and turned her around so that she was sitting. "I wasn't going to do this in the office, I have to admit, but now? Seeing all that beautiful skin of yours?" He slowly unbuttoned his trousers, dropping them to the floor with her skirt and panties, then pulled his shirt over his head. He was thick and soft, like she'd thought, but she had absolutely no doubt that he could push her up against a wall and fuck her until she screamed, if that was what he wanted to do. And she couldn't help eyeing his gorgeous cock; it wasn't particularly long, but it was thick enough that she could anticipate the ache that would come from taking it.

He laughed, soft and rich. "Eyes up here, beautiful." He tapped her gently on the forehead to refocus her attention. "You stare at me like that and I'm going to forget that I'm doing this for you right now." He dropped to his knees, pushed her thighs apart and leaned forward. She expected his mouth, but instead of soft kisses leading up her thigh, he just pulled her clit into his mouth and sucked hard, grazing it with his teeth. The intensity of it was shocking, and she cried out at the sensation lancing through her. The heat of him was gone in a moment; he wasn't even touching her legs. "You're going to get us caught, beautiful, if you can't keep quiet. You have to keep your voice down." He lowered his own voice conspiratorially. "Unless that's what you want. Unless you want to have someone open that door and see you with your assistant's face buried in your cunt. Does that make you want to cum, beautiful?"

"That's...not a particular fantasy of mine at the moment, no." She had to gasp to get the words out, but he'd made her promise.

"Good," he said. "Good, thank you for telling me that. I don't particularly want anyone interrupting us either. Which means you have to be quiet for me. Understand?"

She started to speak, then thought harder, and nodded. His smile lit up and his hands came back to her thighs. She was aching for him, fuck. She couldn't remember the last time she'd felt this needy, this desperate. And he'd hardly touched her.

Of course, there had been two long weeks of nothing but foreplay. It was no wonder she was responding so hard.

His mouth pressed against her again, softer this time. His tongue stroked her once, from her opening to her clit, then softly pulled on her again. "So, here's what we're going to do," he said. "I want that shirt unbuttoned.

I want to see your pretty tits in your matching bra. Don't think I didn't notice. Did you get dressed that way this morning hoping to tease me, beautiful, or just to feel pretty?"

"Pretty," she gasped out between swirls of his tongue around her clit. He moved down, darting inside of her for a second, but moving back before she had anything to rock against. "I wanted to feel pretty."

"And do you?" His hands tightened on her ass, squeezing.

"Yes."

"Good. I'm glad you know what you are." He leaned back for just a moment, considering. He spun the chair so that it was braced against her desk, then guided her so that her feet were braced on his shoulders. She let her knees fall wide, exposing her body to him. Her cheeks flushed hot, but the way he studied her was worth any embarrassment. "So, I'm going to do my very best to make you feel good. You are going to very carefully un-button that blouse. Those buttons look awfully delicate, and if one pops off, I am not going to touch you until you have sewn it back on. Understand?"

"Yes," she said. Her hips were rocking at just the thought of him touching her again, and when his mouth came down on her, setting up a slow rhythm of laps and circles and strokes, she couldn't hold still. Her fingers trembled as she tried to keep control of her hands and carefully work the buttons through their tiny little holes. They suddenly seemed as big as marbles, her fingers thick and clumsy. When had she decided to buy a blouse with so many buttons? She hated herself for it, for every distraction from the swirling, glorious sensation he was causing to swell in her cunt. She couldn't cum like this, she never had, but she was sure she could coast on this wave of pleasure for pretty close to forever.

When the last button came free without any damage, she couldn't contain the sigh of relief. Her hands found the seat of the desk chair and she braced herself a bit more, moving with his eager mouth as he devoured her.

He noticed the change and pulled back again, the lower half of his face soaked with her. "Nicely done, beautiful. Very nice. Do you feel good?"

His thumb flicked over her clit and she cursed. "Yes. Yes. I feel good."

"But you need more to finish, don't you?"

"Yeah." Her cheeks were red hot. She'd had more than a few lovers over the years, but no one had ever been this clear, this direct.

"Tell me what you need."

"I'm...not sure."

That warm, teasing humming. And then his thick first finger slid into her. She was so soaked that there was no resistance at all, but the pleasant sense of penetration and fullness was a beautiful counterpoint to her stimulated clit, currently being tormented by the cold air. He curled his finger gently, testing her until he found that spot that made her twist and grit her teeth to keep from crying out. "Oh beautiful," he said. "I'm sure you can take another one." Another finger pressed into her, and she opened to him easily. Two fingers twisted into her, spreading her wide. "Now," he said, planting a firm kiss on her thigh. "If you want to play with your nipples and your breasts, please do. You only have one job. Okay? Remember not to scream."

She didn't have a chance to agree or say yes before his mouth was on her again, taunting her clit as his fingers worked deep into her, setting up a glorious rhythm that drove her circling up, higher and higher. She lost track of everything but grinding down into his face. Distantly, she knew she was being noisier than she should be, that someone could hear them, but she couldn't help it. She felt herself twisting up, tighter and tighter, her entire body teased up on a pinnacle of need. Her body tightened so hard that she worried she might crush his fingers, but one final stroke inside was the last thing she needed. She just managed to get the heel of her hand between her teeth to keep from screaming as wave after wave of pleasure broke over her. He was making glorious, delighted noises now, too, mirroring her gasps and pants as she wound down, matching her body's slow descent until she went completely liquid and soft. He gathered her up off the chair and pulled her down into his lap, hugging her tight and crooning to her about how beautiful she was, how gorgeous she was, how good she was.

She could feel him, rock hard against her hip, but when she reached for him, he gently directed her hands away. "Not now, beautiful," he said. "In a little while."

She laughed a little and reached again, but this time he moved her hands firmly. "I want you to enjoy yourself too."

He kissed the tip of her nose. "First, having you desperately trying not to scream while you came all over my face was absolutely one of the most enjoyable experiences I've ever had in my life. Second, I'm on a fucking hair trigger right now, and you're way too gorgeous for me to let you think I'm some kind of two-pump chump. A quickie is well and good, but right now, I want to savor you. So, we're going to cool down for a little bit, and then we'll see what happens next." He laughed, just a little, and squeezed her tight. "Want me to make you some coffee?"

She laughed and cuddled against him a little tighter. "If I stay here, I'm going to fall asleep, but if I drink coffee now, I'll be up all night. How would you feel about a shower?"

"There is absolutely zero chance that I'll be naked with you in a shower stall and not end up fucking you. As fun as that sounds, it does lead back to our previous issue and the need to cool off a little. We'll save it for round two."

"So there's going to be a round two?"

He went very still against her. She didn't know what she'd done wrong with her tone, but his voice was close to a whisper. "I hope there's a lot more than two, Olivia. A lot more." The vulnerability in his eyes and his face caught her off guard and she gathered him up in her arms for a moment, just holding him tight. "What about you?" he asked, his tone still carefully neutral.

All the words she knew were stupid. Any version of "me too" sounded like she was only agreeing because he'd said it first. And that softness in his tone, she needed him to know that it was okay. That she was okay with him being like this, too. He could be hard and soft and anything in between. That it was safe.

"I want you," she said, finally. "Whatever that means, whatever that takes. I just want you."

He pulled back, stroking her hair back from her face and searching her eyes. She didn't know what he was looking for, so she just held still, kept herself open and truthful, and let him find what he needed. When he kissed her again, it was sweetest and most passionate thing she'd ever experienced. She managed to turn in his arms to hold him closer. Which led to his cock slotting tidily up against her cunt all over again. He swore into her neck as his cock jumped against her. She pressed herself against him again, but he made a strangled sound, picked up her hips, and pushed her back about six inches. She laughed a little, reveling in how much he wanted her. She wasn't sure anyone had ever wanted her this much.

"You," he said, wagging a finger at her like an old lady, "are not helping, and I'm very sure you're doing it on purpose."

"That's...probably fair, yeah."

He kissed her again, but with a hand on her chest so that she could press closer to him again. "You said you wanted a shower. Why don't you do that, and I'll...sit somewhere quietly and think of very unsexy things. Like clowns. Clowns are absolutely horrifying."

"They are. It's true." She put a little extra wiggle in her hips as she stood, enjoying the way his hand went to his cock, giving himself just a tiny little bit of pressure to relieve some of the ache he seemed to be feeling. She tossed off her blouse and unfastened her bra, dropping them on the office floor, blew him a kiss, then went through the house to shower. She felt awkward as hell; she didn't particularly mind being nude, but she didn't generally traipse around through the house without clothes on, especially when she could hear appreciative noises behind her at the movements of her ass. She half expected him to follow her into the shower after all, but he stopped in her room, stretched out on her bed, and put his hands behind his head. She paused for a moment, studying him. He seemed completely at ease there, his calm and peace only belied by the rigid length of his cock jutting achingly out of his boxer briefs. If she were as turned on as he seemed to be, there were no thoughts in the world that were going to ease the desire. Only ones that would take it all to the boiling point and spill over.

She leaned over and kissed him one more time, doing her best to keep it chaste even with his growl of want and his hand digging into her hair to crush her against him. "Just remember," she managed to say, easing away from him, fully aware of how pretty her tits looked like this. "Even if it's quick. There's going to be Round 2. And 3. And as many as you want."

Something softened in his eyes, and his smile went a little sweet. "I'm looking forward to all the ways I can make you scream."

"Oh, you're not going to tell me to be quiet again?"

He shook his head. "Absolutely not. You're going to be screaming my name, if I have any say in it."

"You will," she said. One more light kiss, because if she didn't back up and get in the shower, she knew she wouldn't.

She turned the water up warm—she wasn't the one claiming she needed to calm down, after all—and ran her hands over her body. It sounded like such a stereotype, but she supposed that, by default, it had to be true sometimes. She'd never had an orgasm like that, never felt herself reach so high and then crash so hard, but even more so, she'd never been held like that. She'd never had someone put aside their own pleasure so that she could focus on hers, because that spiral down was almost as delicious as the journey up. She'd never felt so...well, loved. Before.

It was too soon to use that word. She knew it. That was what got people in trouble, deciding that they were in love after three seconds in each other's company. But his caring for her was so clear. It was intimidating. She'd always wanted romance in the abstract, the stuff you saw on greeting cards and in magazines that specialized in beauty tips and celebrity gossip. Big gestures and grand statements. This idea, that it was the small things, was so bewildering. But of course, wasn't that ultimately what Mr. Darcy had done? Wasn't that the story of most Austen heroines? The small gestures were bigger and more important, and the grand gestures were not always to be trusted.

Jane Austen would have written a story about a man who brought a woman a cup of coffee.

So yeah. Maybe that word...it wasn't time for it yet. But maybe there was something special happening here.

"Olivia? Liv?"

Thomas's voice was sharp and hard, and there was nothing romantic or heated about it.

"Yeah?" She opened the glass door of the shower stall and leaned out.

He looked into the bathroom but didn't really look at her. He was stepping into his pants and pulling his shirt over his head. "I have to go." He started away, then turned back, grabbed her and gave her a kiss that should have been searing hot but was mostly distracted, then pulled away again. Her handprint was wet on his chest, but he didn't seem to notice. "I'm sorry. I have to go. I'll call you. I'm sorry."

And then he was gone.

Olivia let the water run for a long time, trying to keep her tears under control. No, there was no point. She cried in the shower for a while, then got out, dried off, and cried in bed. She found her phone at some point and left it next to her, but there wasn't a ring or a text message. She eventually fell asleep.

Chapter 16

Thomas

Thomas's hands were shaking as he stuffed his laptop back in his bag. He didn't fly much, and getting a ticket had been a hassle, but that wasn't the problem. A few short hours ago, he'd been enjoying everything about the woman he craved so much. He was happy with Olivia, happy in ways that left his soul soothed. He was prepared to show her how much she meant to him, to see where it would go from there. A text from his sister Abby shattered all of it.

Dad had a stroke. He's in the hospital. Come home.

His body had gone numb. Sounds were distorted, it felt like he was moving through water, and even his hurried kiss to Olivia didn't feel as sweet as he'd hoped. The next few hours were a haze of airport Wi-Fi, scrambling between planes for layovers, and frantic messages between him and his three sisters who didn't seem to be handling complete sentences or sharing factual information very well. Hyperfocus had kicked in in a big way, and he pulled it closer. It kept the research out. He started pulling information from different websites about treatments, complications, and outcomes and sorting it into various documents for easy access later. He made a folder on his desktop labeled "Dad - Stroke" and managed not to throw up even a little bit.

He wasn't sure when he'd gotten on that last plane. Against his wishes, he'd finally fallen asleep, and the bump of the wheels hitting the tarmac had sent him into a complete panic. He had a window seat, so he just sat as still as he could while waiting for his heart to stop playing Wagner in his chest. He thought he'd just let the other passengers get off the plane, but after a little while, a flight attendant's voice caught his attention. "Sir?" she said, and probably not for the first time.

"Yeah," he said, trying to gather himself together. He sounded like shit and felt worse, he was almost positive.

"We're on the ground now, and everything's fine. Can I help you with your bag?"

She must have thought he was just a nervous flyer. He managed not to laugh. The idea of everything being fine was beyond comical. He wasn't sure when 'fine' was ever going to be a thing that life was again. Nothing was stable. Nothing was grounded. He thanked her politely, told her that he didn't need help with his bag, and sprinted off the plane.

Elliot Lafayette was waiting for him. He had been a friend of Abby's when she was in high school and had been around their house a lot, though he and Thomas had been too far apart in age to ever really be friends. Apparently, he and Abby were still good enough friends for a "pick my brother up at the airport that's 50 miles away' favor. That was good; he'd like Elliot. Something had happened during his and Abby's senior year that had driven them apart, but they'd been good together, and he'd always had a secret hope that the two of them would get together.

Elliot was broad-shouldered and stocky, and even at 4am, he had an easy and compassionate smile. He had on the same plaid flannel shirt that he'd been wearing in high school. He reached out to shake Thomas's hand and grab the carry-on bag he'd run home and grabbed before catching his flight. "Sorry it's like this," he said, New England reserve thick in his voice. "Need some coffee on the way to the hospital?"

Olivia probably would have made them coffee in the morning. Explained to him all the different types of coffee she could make and expected him to choose.

"Yeah, that would be good," Thomas said. When you can't make your own energy anymore, store bought was fine.

While his family lived about 50 miles away from Burlington, his father's stroke had apparently been severe enough that the local hospital had decided to send him to the "major" hospital in the state, a comical statement when he'd spent years living near Boston General and then George Washington Medical Center. Elliot found them a 24-hour gas station that he promised would have better coffee than the hospital, and he bought a couple of snacks and sodas as well. Who knew if his sisters had been eating at all?

Back in the car, Thomas resisted the urge to do a little more research on his phone on the rest of the drive. He'd already combed through all the official and quasi-official medical sites, if he went much further, he was going to be looking at snake oil and faith healing. That would just make him mad, and right now, he would probably fall for anything. "Did Abby tell you anything?"

Elliot shook his head. "Not really. She said your dad was on the way to the hospital, and could I please pick you up. Texted me your flight info."

"Well, thanks for coming all this way."

"Not a problem."

"You coming into the hospital?"

"Nah, family only for visitors right now. Abby...nah. She'll call me later if she wants to."

There was a tone there that Thomas was too tired to dig into or try to understand. "Want me to keep you updated on what happens?"

It was a reach of a question, but his guess panned out. Elliot's knuckles whitened as he gripped the steering wheel harder. "I'd appreciate it."

He had no idea what had happened between Elliot and Abby, but he could bet it wasn't good. "Okay," he said. Another few minutes passed in silence and Thomas found himself sighing. "Sorry I'm not much company right now. I've been doing research on side-effects, long-term effects, likely complications. I know the doctors will give us information, but..." he knew the rest of the sentence. *My sisters were there when it happened, they're probably in shock. I left, and I didn't have to go through that, and I'm the one who can handle this part best anyway. I have to.* Instead of saying any of that, he went with "Well, you know how it is."

Elliot tapped the steering wheel a few times, keeping his gaze focused ahead instead of forcing him to accept the emotions of someone who was basically a stranger. "You're a good son, Thomas. I know you can handle it."

Thomas held on to that. He doubted he'd be hearing much of that come the next few days.

They pulled up to the hospital, and he got out of the car. Vernon reminded him of his bags – Thomas felt like he'd forget anything that wasn't in front of his face right now. Almost anything, at least. He sent Olivia a quick text for luck.

My dad's in the hospital. I landed. Contact you soon.

He hesitated briefly. He should say more. He'd promised to fuck her until she was screaming, then abandoned her in the shower. He needed to say more. Five different half-formed thoughts, all threaded through with confused emotions that he wasn't entirely ready to share, swam through his head. He missed her. He wanted her here. This was a nightmare. The thought of her was keeping him upright. She was incredible. Whatever came next, he was here for it. Business or otherwise. He wanted to be there.

I'll work remotely. Not leaving. Just need to be here for them.

He thought about adding more, about the feelings that had been developing for weeks and that he now knew to be real. He thought about calling her and letting loose about how he had never been a good enough son, never done the right things. He'd never gotten it right. So, he had to be here, had to do this, had to take the weight off his sisters. He had to be the strong one.

Instead, he put his phone on 'do not disturb' and dropped it in his pocket.

The hospital was horrible, as hospitals always were, and it took him a few minutes to wind his way up to the medical intensive care unit where his father currently was. The waiting room was small, and it was mostly full of his sisters. Sharon, the tallest and oldest, was white as a sheet. Ellie was urgently hush-shouting into her phone, pacing facing frantically, the words "a short leave of absence, please" the only thing he could make out. And Abby, God love her, seemed to have cornered a nurse on the other side of the waiting room. Her voice had that particular squeak it got when she was terrified but was convinced she was being a pinnacle of logic.

"Are you seriously telling me that I can't agree to medical treatments for my unconscious father because of paperwork?"

The nurse looked beyond weary. He wondered how long she'd been working, how many times she'd repeated herself, and how many things she needed to do other than this. "I'm sorry," she said. "I promise you, we're taking good care of him. You said you got ahold of his medical proxy, and that he should be here soon—"

Abby's sharp laugh cut him to the core. "Yeah, we'll see if he even bothers to show up. I need to know that we can take care of Dad now, not if Thomas bothers to answer my phone calls."

Thomas had planned to start with hugging, but any chance of that was gone now. "Hi, Abby," he said, gently moving her to the side and catching the nurse's attention. "I got on the actual next plane after I got your message. What's going on?" He liked to think of himself as a patient and soft-spoken man, but right now, he didn't trust himself with anything. He dug his hand into the strap of his bag so hard that his knuckles were probably white. He had to fight down his own panic and fear and sort this out. Abby had handled enough.

"Swooping in to save the day, huh?" Abby made a furious sound and spun away from them. Thomas wondered how many more times tonight he'd remind himself that Abby was good in an immediate crisis and then fell apart in the aftermath, that she struggled at accepting help, that she felt a responsibility to take care of things even though she was the youngest, and that she didn't handle it well when something was outside of her sphere of ability. When they got out of this—he refused to allow himself to make that conditional, even in his head —and there was a mountain of paperwork to deal with, Abby would shine. Sharon would organize anything that needed to happen at the house, and Ellie would leverage every connection Dad had ever had to make sure they all had whatever they needed. Frankly, they'd always had all the angles covered, and Thomas had always been superfluous to the system.

After all, it was normally his dad who filled the role of "the calm in the storm."

Well, time to step up.

The nurse was watching him warily. Probably wondering if there was going to be someone new shouting the same things. He put on a concerned-but-calm expression, the farthest thing he could imagine from how he actually felt, but the only option he had. "What's going on that a medical proxy is needed?"

"Nothing right now," the nurse said. "The stroke was significant, but the surgery went well, and that's a good sign in itself. I had just asked your sister if they'd been able to contact you because you were listed as the medical proxy. She...had some concerns."

That was generous.

"I'm sorry for the confusion. I didn't know Dad listed me." Or, really, what that would mean. "I'll be here. If anything does come up."

The nurse nodded. "You should be able to come in and see him soon. I'll come and let you know once he's settled. It'll probably just be one or two people at a time at first, so. Please be prepared for that." The nurse had clearly identified them as the family most likely to ruin her shift, and he couldn't blame her. She vacated the room before anyone else could attack her over things that she couldn't control.

He turned to his sisters, who were all watching him. "Hi. Nice to see you guys."

It was supposed to be funny. Not cause them all to burst into tears. Including him. But hey, if a guy couldn't cry while his father was in the hospital after a major heart attack, when could he?

The four of them wrapped each other up in some kind of awkward hug pile that had always happened when things got really out of control. He was at the center, holding Abby as she fell apart. Sharon and Ellie wrapped their arms around him and Abby, protecting their younger siblings as best as they could.

When they'd all cried themselves out—at least a little —he sat down to Google what the fuck it was that a medical proxy did.

The next few hours were a blur. There had been damage it might last, it might not. There wasn't any way to tell right now. Dad would probably need rehab. The house would need to be adapted to be more accessible. He couldn't move his left arm well and his left leg almost at all. When Dad was conscious, he cracked jokes about how that was fine, he hadn't gone dancing since Mom died. He seemed confused that no one else was laughing.

Over the next week, he and his sisters took turns at the hospital, keeping their father company, trying to adjust. The physical damage that the stroke had done was clear and obvious. The mental changes were harder to anticipate. His dad seemed to have lost some verbal filters; he'd never been a particularly emotionally vulnerable man, but he was talking about Mom now in a way that made Thomas ache. Sharon, the only one of them who remembered Mom really well, couldn't handle it at all, and he and Abby had been so young when she died that it was like their father was talking about a stranger. Ellie kept interjecting with the few memories she had, which made Sharon cry harder.

Thomas did his best to be the rock. He worked with the rehab doctors to make sure he understood what modifications would need to be made, then talked to Abby so that she could put her incredible skills to work and start revamping the inside of the house. Dad's bedroom was moved downstairs, a ramp to the porch was built and a pathway was paved so that a wheelchair could get around. Thankfully none of the doors needed to be widened. Sharon and Ellie were working out a schedule as to who would be at the house when to make sure Dad wasn't alone and figuring out when they would need to hire someone to be there. Ellie's leave, of course, had not been approved, and she was snappish at everyone because she wanted to help more than she could. So Thomas told them that he could stay for a while. A knot was in his stomach when he said it, but he made himself mean it.

He did his best to keep up with Olivia. He tried to keep track of her schedule and keep her from double-booking herself, but without being in the office, there was little he could do beyond damage control. He could see things spiraling out of control again, people going back to their habits of emailing people randomly instead of using the company software and internal messaging. And he texted Olivia when he could, but he struggled to think of what to say. He was in such an intense, focused place, trying to keep up with his sisters and his dad. When he thought of her, all he could remember how beautiful she'd looked when he'd kissed her in the shower before bolting out the door—and wondering if she'd ever trust him to be near her again. Her messages seemed distant, controlled. Cautious. And could he really blame her? With all the push and pull she'd clearly been going through, convincing herself that he was off limits then daring herself to give in, over and over—how could she possibly be okay? But the few times he tried to open that line of conversation, she shut it down, telling him not to worry about her.

In the spare time he had, he worked on the Small and Sparkling app. He had no idea if Olivia would ever want to use it at this point, but it was like an itch that he needed to scratch. He wasn't good at getting projects half done, and even if this wasn't the next big thing that established him as a serious programmer, he'd always be able to use it as a potential portfolio piece. He was going to get the cool thing done so he could make the next cool thing.

Thomas's old room at the house had been turned into a guest room, which was both fitting and helpful; sleeping in the room with all his teenage memorabilia would have been weird. And it was better than Ellie's room, which had become an exercise room that was, of course, never used. There were good odds that Sharon had actually been the one to set it up, convinced Dad would use it if it was there. The layers of dust implied that he never had.

He laid back on the uncomfortable bed and tried to breathe. He didn't know how long he was going to be in this small town. He'd already run away from it once, and the circumstances of his return were not making it more appealing. He wanted to be back in the city, in the busyness and the activity and the press of people. He wanted to be back with specific people.

He was dialing her number before he noticed the time. It was well past midnight, and he went to press disconnect, prepped to follow up with an "oops, I didn't notice the time" text, but she answered before he could.

"Thomas?" The word was tangled up in a yawn, but she didn't sound like she'd been sleeping. He got a notification that the user was trying to switch to a video call, and he accepted, turning the bedside lamp on so she'd be able to see him and not just a creepy face out of a bad horror movie. He could see her in a brightly lit room.

The living room, he thought. Her hair was mussed and there were circles under her eyes. She looked surprised, but her voice sounded happy. "Hi. I didn't expect you to call."

He smiled and couldn't remember the last time he'd really smiled. Probably not since Abby's text. "Hi. I didn't realize what time it was. You're still up?"

"Yeah. Extra late last minute edits."

Half of her day had theoretically been empty. What had he missed? "I'm sorry. How are you holding up?"

She waved off his concern. "I'm fine. How's your dad? How are you?"

He knew his smile was weak. "Dad's getting better. I'm...fine." The words about wanting to be with her, wanting to be close to her and find out what kind of body wash she used as he helped her get clean after bouts of increasingly vigorous sex, about wanting to hold her after while she fell asleep, they were all too much. Too much to say when he was here, not there, and when he couldn't react based on what she said. "We're all managing."

"That's good." There was a long pause, and he could see a million emotions running across her face, but he couldn't tease them out. Whether she was regretting what had happened. He couldn't get a lock on it.

"Yeah," he said, aiming for the infodump to avoid the silence. "It's seeming like Dad's going to be semi-mobile, and we don't know how much rehab will help, though he's doing well so far. Abby's been working on converting the house to make it accessible, but he's going to be home in a few days, so there's a lot to do. We're trying to find someone to come and help him out with...you know, the stuff that he can't do on his own, but it's not easy. But we're making it work." "Yeah. Does that mean," she yawned a little, but he could practically see her shaking it off. God, he wanted to tuck her into bed more than anything. "That you'll be there for a while?"

"Maybe. I don't know. I've been working on the app, you know. It's pretty close to done. I gave myself access to an old build of your database, so I can work with a version of the stories and try and get it up and running. It won't be a full version of anything, but I think you'll be impressed by what I've got here."

"You don't to have to worry about that now," she said. "I don't know if we'll even be able to use it. So there's no need to worry about it."

The brushoff hurt, even if she didn't mean it that way. "I'm not worried about it." Concern crossed her face and he cursed himself. "I mean, it's something to focus on that's normal." There were words he hadn't been able to say to his sisters. He knew they saw it too, but their father had never been weak, and they didn't know how to talk about it anymore than he did. "They say there's no cognitive damage, but he's different. He's talking about our mother and being...different. Sharon, my oldest sister, she's falling apart constantly, and I swear Abby's going to try and beat me up one of these days, even though she's half my size and I'm not actually the problem. I'm managing all of them, but it's just hard, Liv. It's hard."

"Then," she paused, and her voice changed. Soft and gentle. "Then you should focus on what you need to do. With everything you've done here, I can coast off inertia for a while. I understand you need to be where you are."

I need you, he didn't say. He couldn't tell if she was pushing him away or trying to be comforting. The ambiguity didn't help much. But he answered her words and let that be enough. "You'll call me if you need me though."

"I promise not to take up your time on this. You don't have to worry about me."

I want to worry about you, he didn't say. God, how had she gotten so wound in his head? "Not a question, Olivia. Just trust me." Everything that would have come after that was too much, and definitely more than he wanted to say on a phone call. "Look, I have to go, I don't know when I'll get any sleep next. I just needed to talk to you."

"Needed to?" Her tone was neutral, but not unwelcoming.

He took a leap. "After everything, I just left, and it wasn't what I wanted. I didn't want to go, I just couldn't stay after I got that text, and I ran. I didn't run from you. I'm not running. Promise me you know that."

The silent pause was agonizing. Her voice, when she spoke, was just as neutral. "I promise, Thomas. And don't worry. I can take care of myself. You can call or text me when you want to, just – remember what's important, that's all. Goodnight."

"Goodnight, Liv."

"Liv, huh?" There was a bit of a laugh in her tone. He'd been close to hanging up, but he pushed himself away from the sleep that was suddenly threatening to overwhelm him.

"Yeah. Sorry, it just kind of happened, in my head. Do you...like it? Want me to stop?"

"No, it's..." she smiled, and it was more of a smile than anything else in this whole stupid conversation. "No one's ever tried out a nickname before."

"It's Liv or beautiful. Or both. Beautiful Liv." He remembered how she'd tasted, and he wanted to kiss her again more than he wanted to breathe.

"I like it," she said, and he was going to hang onto that smile for days. "Goodnight, Thomas."

"Goodnight, beautiful Liv," he said, and got to hear her laughing as she hung up the phone. He fell back on his bed. She had been nothing but sweet to him. She'd laughed at his offering of a pet name for her. She'd seemed happy to talk to him. So why did it feel like his heart had gotten ripped out of his chest? He sighed, ignored how hard he was, thinking about all the things he hadn't done with her yet, and tried to get some sleep.

Chapter 17

Olivia

Olivia dropped her cell phone onto her desk and put her head in her hands. She wasn't being fair. Thomas had needed to race home, several states away, because his father had a stroke. He needed to be there for his family. The way he was talking about them, it didn't seem like he had a particularly good relationship with his family. Not a horribly bad one, either, but not one where he would have a weekly standing phone call with his sister or plan visits back home outside of Christmas. There was something he was holding back, something he wasn't saying. It seemed like it was eating at him. And with him being so distant...even though it made sense, even though she knew he should be focused on other things, she couldn't help worrying that maybe he was regretting what had happened between them.

Which wasn't fair to either of them. They'd had sex one time. Granted, it had been really, really good sex. But

174

it wasn't like he'd asked her to marry him or anything. Maybe that was why—

No. No, she wasn't going to let herself go down some self-pitying train where she tried to convince herself that she wasn't worth enough for him to pay attention to her after...well, he hadn't even gotten off. But maybe he hadn't been satisfied with what did happen. Hell, maybe he'd come in his fist after she'd gotten in the shower and had decided that was enough. Maybe he even thought it was for her own good. Was he doing some kind of noble thing, where if he just put her at enough distance, she could see that he wasn't the man for her?

Olivia. Get a damn grip. Life is not a romance novel. She tried to imagine Lydia's voice in her head. Her little sister, who had been so swept up by every pretty face that ran by when she was young, and who was now so distant and distracted and just...sad. That was the problem. Lydia had been so sad the last few times they'd talked. It was disorienting, like true north had just shifted. It didn't make sense. None of it made sense. *He wouldn't still be calling you beautiful and giving you nicknames if he was regretting everything that happened. Breathe.*

She was overreacting. She knew it. She'd been grateful for his phone call not just because it meant she got to talk to him, but because he had distracted her from the fear spiral brought on by Jenny Lawson's phone call earlier that day. Where she'd said that she'd had enough of Small and Sparkling's mistakes over the past month. That might be enough to shutter her company for good.

"You have to understand," Jenny had said. "It's nothing personal. You've always been great to me, Olivia. You supported this story when everyone else said it was too sweeping, too overwhelming, too daytime TV. But that one mistake—this wasn't a misplaced comma or a their where there should have been a they're." Somehow, Olivia could perfectly understand which homonym went where in Jenny's sentence. It was an actual magic trick. She was sure of it.

"I know, I feel terrible about it," Olivia said, trying to convey all of her misery and guilt for the way her company was going to pieces into two short phrases.

"I know you do." Jenny sounded like a mother reassuring her child that it was all going to be okay, but they still had to clean up the milk they'd spilled. "And I know that S&S has done everything to try and fix it. I appreciate the advertising credits, and you fixed the mistake minutes after I called. But it was made in the first place. Someone got a screenshot and it went viral on one of the video platforms. I'm still getting angry messages from people who've been 'reading for years' and are 'so betrayed I could do such a thing.'" This grumble was almost to herself. "If they were so distraught over it, you'd think they'd come and see the fix and the gratuitous groveling I did about the mistake." Then, her attention was focused on Olivia again. "Do you know that I got an email telling me that I should go and read *Misery* so I would understand what happened to authors who didn't behave. Can you imagine?"

What was she supposed to say? 'Jesus, that's messed up.' 'Wow, you're getting threats based on forty-year-old horror novels, what the hell?' 'Do you think they read the book or watched the movie?' "Oh god, I'm so sorry." She could try and say that Small and Sparkling would release an apology, but they'd already done that, and they'd make sure she'd be featured in the next print version, and ... but there was no 'and' good enough right now.

In another world, one where she was better rested and less terrified, Olivia was pretty sure she could have come up with a different solution. Now, there wasn't a lot to do but grovel. "It'll never happen again. I'll check every chapter myself." Because she had time for that. It didn't matter. She'd sleep a little less. *I'm not going to be getting laid any time soon, apparently.*

Olivia was not normally inclined toward self-violence, but the intrusive thoughts were starting to get a little bit much. She took a deep breath and prepared for another round of offers-slash-begging-for-forgiveness.

Before she could, Jenny let out a big dramatic sigh. "None of that is why I'm calling, though." Oh shit. There was a tone there, a kind of 'I'm so sorry we won't be able to go to the circus, dear, Mommy has to work' tone that made her nervous. "I've been working on this story for years now, and a lot of readers still love it, but...it's long. I've done my best to make jumping on and jumping off points depending on why people have turned up, but...it was the *Misery* comment that actually got me. I'm tired of this world. I don't have much new to do with it. I think it's time to try something else."

Olivia's heart started to beat a little faster. Was this...hope? A new story by Jenny Lawson—she could see how to use it, attract new fans, excite new people, up subscriptions. "That's great—"

"But I think that it might be a good idea for me to try it somewhere else."

The idea of hope deflating made it seem like it was a gradual process, and saying that it burst implied a violence that Olivia didn't feel. Instead, it was just an instant flatness, a lack of emotion that left a world of exhaustion in its wake. "Jenny—"

But it was clear that Jenny Lawson had a speech prepared, and there was no room in it for turn-taking. "It wasn't just this single mistake. I want to make sure that's clear. And I don't want to be the canary in the coal mine here, but it's seemed for a while that S&S has just kind of...stalled. I know you're doing a great job bringing on new people and expanding the kinds of stories you're telling. I hate being the person who's saying 'what have you done for me lately?' but—"

"But here you are." That was cold. It wasn't what someone said to their biggest draw, their biggest asset, their keystone. But the words had knocked her back in her chair, and she had to work to breathe.

"I'm being fully honest here, and I hope that counts for something. I'm being courted by other companies.

And they have more going for them. I appreciate the changes you've been making to make it easier for authors to get access to the staff and editors, but it's...these are changes that other people made five years ago. I wish I could tell you that I was in this for the art or something ridiculous like that, Olivia, but you're the one who told me—"

"That what I wanted to do was make it so that your writing paid the bills. And that you had to go where the money was." She remembered that conversation clearly. The context had been different. She'd been convincing Jenny that starting off with a couple that was just a little bit nontraditional and then incorporating more and more diverse elements over time once she'd built an audience was going to be key.

"And I need to do that," Jenny said. "I'm still thinking it through. I don't want to make any rash decisions. You've made my career, Olivia, you and S&S, and I don't want you to think I don't know that. You deserve to know I'm thinking about it."

For a lot of people, it would have been an attempt to gain a bargaining chip or some other kind of leverage. For Jenny, it was just honesty and integrity. "I appreciate that," Olivia said. She felt completely numb. "Would you please let me know if there's anything I can do to sway your decision? I know you need to go where your career takes you, and I don't want to hold you back. But if there's something I can give you, some way we can continue to work together, I want to do that."

"I appreciate that," Jenny said, and it sounded sincere. "I'll stay in touch."

The call disconnected. Hours later, sitting in her living room and still panicked, she'd gotten Thomas's call. She'd done her best to keep things light, calm, focused on him and his needs because hers were too overwhelming, and even if he was here, he couldn't fix them, so the last thing she'd wanted to do was make him worry about something else he couldn't do.

Thinking back over the conversation, she could only hear the things she hadn't said. Had her insisting that he take the time he needed sounded like a brush off? Had she seemed so needy and desperate that he didn't think she could take care of herself? Was that why he'd wanted to be so sure she'd go running to him for help? Was he thinking about that night at all?

All the thoughts she didn't have time for were choking her. She picked up her phone again, desperate to say something, anything, so he'd know that things were okay. She typed and deleted three messages before getting to

Sorry if I was distant. Work is crazy. I'm glad you called.

A long pause. Then she added

I miss you.

Clearly, he left her on read because he was already almost asleep. She didn't allow herself to think of any other reason.

Chapter 18

Olivia

Two weeks after Jenny Lawson had told her that she was going to abandon the sinking ship previously known as Small and Sparkling, after 14 days of awkward texts and occasional phone calls with Thomas where the only sign of intimacy was that he kept calling her Liv, Olivia still had absolutely no idea what to do about anything that was happening in her life. The office was chaos. The new systems Thomas had implemented were great, but he hadn't had the opportunity to create documentation or training before he had to leave. The people who easily adapted to systems like these were using them and loving them. Those who did not intuitively understand a multi-functional system for document transmission, group chats, message threads, and content management were struggling, and Olivia didn't know how to help. Work was being duplicated everywhere, and no one seemed to have a clue what was going on. Callie had tried to take point on all of that, keeping the editors and the programmers and customer service all talking to each other, but with so many remote workers and so few people agreeing on the best way to talk, she was at her wit's end. So asking Callie to try and manage her calendar wasn't going to happen.

So, Olivia had gone back to trying to manage her own calendar. The problem was that she'd never really been good at it, which was why she'd hired an assistant years ago. He'd been fine (apart from the closet episode), but then she'd had two blissful weeks of having someone do an amazing job of laying out her daily schedule and to-dos, and now she was even more unsure of how to get things done than she'd had before. She was sure there were undotted Ts and crossed Is everywhere, but she couldn't find them in the endless notifications and emails. With more time, she was sure she would have figured out what Thomas was doing and could have applied some of the lessons without thinking about it too much. But right now, it was hard to commit to changing things when she knew it was a matter of time. She knew she needed to start making phone calls, start trying to arrange...something, anything, so she wouldn't take everyone down with her when S&S finally sank. Even if the concept made her feel like she was going to throw up.

She'd spent most of her morning trying to untangle a knot of triple booking herself on Friday morning, so when there was a knock on her open door just after

11, when she thought her schedule was supposed to be empty, she couldn't muster too much surprise.

She looked up to see a tall, classically handsome man with dark hair organized in a stylish swoop back from his forehead standing in her office doorway. It took a moment for her to place him, but after a second, her brain caught up. Mason Baudrier. Callie's best friend, Thomas's roommate, and—most relevant to her—on the board or a prominent member of several of the local business organizations. He was a well-known angel investor in the community, and, in the few interactions she'd had with him, he seemed like a decent guy.

She had absolutely no idea why he was here. "Mason," she said, standing up and extending her hand. "I'm sorry, things are a bit chaotic around here this week. Big launch coming up." Lie. "I was excited to see you on my calendar." Double lie. "How can I help you?"

She gestured toward the chair across from her desk, and he sat down. He had the kind of aura that owned a room; she felt more than a little intimidated in her own office. That thought had both her mental-Thomas and mental-Lydia breathing down her neck, and she forced herself to straighten up a little bit.

Mason was watching her closely. "I wanted to know how things were working out with Thomas. Have you heard from him lately?"

Wasn't Thomas his roommate? She thought that was how Callie had known him in the first place. If so, why hadn't Thomas been talking to him? "We've talked occasionally. He's doing well here. He's been...giving me a fresh perspective on why some of the things that have been shaky around here have been so shaky." Too little too late, probably, given that her first and most prolific and well-known writer was abandoning ship. *No. No descending into grief and misery. Not now.*

Mason nodded. "Word has definitely gotten around that Small and Sparkling is doing some reorganizing. I think it's great that you're taking advantage of some of the assets the business community has to offer smaller companies."

She nodded. "I really had no idea what was available. I wish I'd seen some of it sooner."

"Yeah, I hear you. We put together a mentorship program a long time ago, but there wasn't a lot of interest. Everything about this," he gestured to take in her office, the company, the world. "Is overwhelming."

Given that Mason oversaw a multi-billion dollar investment company, his comment could have been incredibly condescending. He sold it though, somehow, making her feel seen instead of belittled. "I remember there was something when I first opened," Olivia said. "But I didn't...know how to take advantage of it."

"That makes sense," he said, considering his words carefully. "So maybe a mentorship program that specifically picks up after you've been open for a bit, helps you see what's out there once you have a better idea of what you need. That makes a lot of sense. I'll float that around."

He was definitely the kind of guy who made you feel heard regardless of what you were saying. She was pretty sure right now that she could tell him about her latest discovery that two plus two equaled four, and he'd be thrilled for her. He might clap. And be utterly fucking sincere about it.

It was obviously a superpower. One she wanted for herself. Dammit.

"I wanted to check in, though. See what's going on around here."

Now his tone seemed a bit firmer. "You say that like you think something *is* going on. Beyond my getting a new assistant. I don't really know what you're asking."

"Are you deliberately trying to get the company to a lean state in preparation for selling?" He said the words without much inflection, like he'd asked if she was going to step out for lunch after their meeting.

That rocked her back in her chair. "What are you talking about?"

Mason shrugged, his tone staying nonjudgmental. "What it looks like externally is that, very suddenly, you've started completely reorganizing how you're doing business, from internal and external communications to publishing practices to marketing attempts. Those are the things that a small business does when it's starting to prep for sale or going public and wants to look as attractive as possible. There's nothing about your company as it stands that would benefit it from being publicly traded, so it follows that you might be thinking of selling." He flashed a wicked grin that, if she hadn't had Thomas so heavily on her mind, would have caught her attention in a big way. "And if you are, I want in."

In a different world, Olivia would have had some kind of snappy comeback. She would have laughed it off, or told him that he was imagining things, or that S&S was doing better than ever. She would have even told him that Thomas was executing everything based on her initiative, and that they were ready to launch a brand new phase of the company.

In this world, however, she started to cry. She pressed the heels of her hands into her eyes as if that would somehow stop the tears from flowing, but that did nothing. At least she was able to prevent herself from letting out an ugly sob. Her nose running, though? That was going to be inevitable in five...four...three...two...yeah, there it was. *Fuck.*

She heard Mason stand and expected him to...no, she didn't know what. To snap at her to get it together, or stop out of the office to tell the world that she was too emotional to run a business, or some other damn thing? She heard his footsteps move towards her door and then...gently close it. He walked back to her desk, grabbed a container of tissues that were on a shelf—she truly had no idea how long they had been there—and passed them to her. And then he was quiet, waiting.

When the worst of the storm had passed, she took a deep breath and tried to collect herself. Yes, she'd just had a breakdown in front of one of the most major players in the DC business scene. But he was also the best friend of two of her favorite people. That combination of things might actually make him...helpful to her, right now.

"I doubt I could sell this company right now even if I wanted to, and I don't want to," she said, still sniffling a little. She tried to hold her dignity, then gave up and blew her nose. As anticipated, it was an awful, snotty sound, but she could breathe a little better. It gave her room to steady her breathing and dab under her eyes. She hadn't worn much makeup today, so messy mascara was possible, but not the world's biggest problem. Redness and puffiness, however, were unavoidable. "The truth is that we're sinking, and it seems like we're sinking faster every day."

Mason leaned in, his hands together between his knees, and his face seeming open and serious. "Tell me what's going on."

"I'm not entirely sure," she said, honestly. "It's like things have stagnated, but I don't know why. We've got new stories coming out, new authors, people still seem excited on the company's socials, but nothing's growing. Thomas suggested—and he's probably right, he's clearly a tech guy—that our shitty systems were part of the problem. So he was working on getting that...I don't know, that propellor running, to stretch a metaphor."

"But now he's with his family."

"Now he's with his family, and with things half implemented, it's worse than ever. But it's not just that. There have been little mistakes and little slowdowns, but we had a major meltdown with our biggest author a few weeks back—it sounds silly, but one little name change and her entire fanbase wanted to eat her alive—and now she's considering changing to another publisher. If I lose her..." she shrugged. "Then I might as well just wrap things up as best as I can, because she can take her entire series with her. I could probably convince her to give me three months with the backlist, but the odds of her wanting to split her audience's attention like that?"

"Right, from a branding perspective it would be an absolute nightmare." Mason thought for a moment. "So, what ground haven't you explored?"

"What?"

"Tell me about the business. If you had all the money in the world, what would you do with it?"

The question didn't make sense in her head.

When her silence stretched, he tried a different one. "Do you see opportunities for the business to grow in new ways?"

"I wish I could," she said, rubbing a hand over her forehead. "I feel like an idiot because I can't. It's all just such a tangled, hellish morass of stuff. I could cut a ton of staff, but I don't think it'll help long-term, it'll just stretch out the time it takes us to die. I'm missing something, and I can't figure it out." A half conversation played back in her head. "Frankly, the only thing I've ever thought of was an app. When we started out, all the novel and writing sites were just that, websites. A bunch of them put out apps a few years ago, but all the apps are the same. I couldn't ever figure out how to make mine stand out, and the benefits just aren't clear for us. And they're expensive to develop..."

"And the lead time is long, and you're already struggling." Mason rubbed his chin like he was thinking, but there was something in his eyes that was...surprising. She couldn't quite figure it out. Like he knew something she didn't. "Have you considered angel investments? Give you the capital you'd need to stay afloat while something was developed?"

"Angel investors always want a chunk of profits or control in the company. I started Small and Sparkling with a very specific concept, and...by avoiding having real erotica on the platform, I know I've handicapped us some. It's a huge driver for most readers, and letting them go somewhere else to find it loses me dollars, but trying to pivot and include that now would feel like selling out. Small and Sparkling wouldn't be...well, what it is." She thought harder and then sighed. "And we don't just allow queer content, and not just bi girls who date men or very specific types of gay stories. I've pushed for a really inclusive space where people are honored, and where stories are written by people who have a community connection to them. I'm worried an investor would push to stop that. I know those readers aren't our biggest spenders, but god, they are loyal. But someone only looking at the bottom line might not see that."

"So, you'd have to find an investor you could really trust."

"Yes."

"And someone who was willing to sign and say that they wouldn't have any kind of actual control or profit share until you sold the business or went public."

She scoffed. "That would be a shitty investment. Who would even do that?"

"Me."

She couldn't help it; she burst out laughing. "Why?"

"It probably sounds corny, but I believe in what you're doing here. I don't want to see you fail. And that's not just because you employ two of my best friends." That bright grin again, and she again wondered why on earth Callie wasn't dating him.

"I'm not kidding. This would be a terrible investment. I don't even know how much capital it would take to keep us afloat for the—what, year? Eighteen months?—that it would take to get an app up and running."

"We could take a look at the books and figure it out, but you're not all that big of a company, Olivia. It would look like a ton of money to you but, and I'm sorry if this is rude, but I doubt very much it would look like much to me." He held up a hand to forestall whatever she was going to say next. "Look, I didn't come here to steamroll you or try to convince you to do something you didn't want to do. If you're not comfortable with it, you're not, and I'll respect that. But you should know," he said, as he stood. "That I didn't have an appointment. Make sure to check your calendar, and if someone down as supposed to be here right now, you'll want to follow up on that." His tone was kind, even if the words felt like shit. He walked out the door without saying anything more.

Olivia looked at the disaster that was her calendar, her email, and her bullet journal, then grabbed her little makeup bag out of her purse and went to the bathroom to try and clean up whatever damage she'd done with her crying jag. Whatever happened next, she was going to do her best to face it with great eyeliner.

Chapter 19

Olivia

When Olivia saw the appointment scheduled on her calendar, she snorted out a laugh. "Tits&Ass – Campagna's" was absolutely not something she'd written down. If Thomas had been in the office, she would have bet he was trying to make her laugh, but then the actual entry would have included information like who the hell she was meeting and why she was meeting them. She certainly hadn't entered the meeting. Maybe Callie had, or maybe it was actually someone else's secret rendezvous that had gotten entered on her calendar because no one seemed to have a damn idea how to run anything at this exact moment. Including her. She sent Callie a message asking if this was her doing but got no response.

Oh, what the hell. She was hungry. She was in the mood for chicken parm. Someone would show up or they wouldn't, and either way, she'd have lunch.

On her way to the restaurant, she tried to run through potential meetings in her head. It would be weird for Callie to have set up something with a new author. Callie knew better than anyone how S&S was teetering on the edge of collapse. Bringing in someone new, unless it was damn Nora Roberts or something, wasn't a great idea. She'd seen the backlash that happened when a publisher brought on a new author and then immediately folded. Not only did it throw the writer's life into the spin cycle, it made the publisher look like crap, which then reflected on everyone else who'd ever published with them.

But the alternatives didn't make any more sense. There wasn't anyone in the business community that she was going to sit down with right now, they needed new editors or artists even less than they needed new writers, and if there was other staff who were going to be brought on, they would be hired by someone else. So what the hell was this meeting?

She'd made up her mind that it had to be a mistake on her calendar, but when she got to the restaurant, she still let the hostess know that someone might be looking for her. She was several minutes early, and she committed to waiting fifteen minutes; if no one showed up by then, she'd just eat and head back to the office. Wait for the deus ex machina that would save her business for her.

For a moment, she let herself imagine having Thomas there with her. She was trying so hard not to miss him too much. He was busy, taking care of his family, and it was what he should be doing right now. But she'd gotten so used to him so quickly, and being in his arms that night had felt so right. She couldn't help but believe that they had a chance at something special, but with him gone, it seemed like it was slipping away. Just the thought of it made her stomach do unpleasant flips.

She was distracted from her maudlin troubles, however, when the most garish human being she'd ever seen outside of a music video walked into the restaurant. He was tall, middle aged, a bit thick in the middle. He had dark brown hair that was straight out of the late 90s with its blond frosted tips. His suit jacket was some kind of purple and yellow paisley abomination, and his pants were pinstriped. He was wearing round sunglasses with yellow glass frames and had a cheesy goatee that looked like it was made of felt. "Olivia Michaelson," he said to the hostess, his voice about a thousand times louder than it needed to be. "I'm meeting her for lunch."

Oh god, no. She recognized the voice. Granted, the only time she'd heard it, she had someone teasing her nipples with his fingers while she ground her ass into his cock, but it had been distinctive all the same. Evan Lowry looked just as loud and obnoxious as he sounded.

When he'd been on the phone, she'd been pleasantly distracted and wanted to avoid burning bridges. Today, she was too tired for...for any of whatever he represented. She'd spent more time searching him online after that phone call. Between the "where's titties" game he'd gotten the internet playing with his dragons and queens show and the way he'd boned an extra who immediately became a recurring character on the show, he was everything she was opposed to in modern media. And his jacket was making her dizzy.

As the hostess led him toward her table, Olivia stood. "Mr. Lowry," she said as he turned and slipped a folded up hundred dollar bill to the hostess, whose eyes immediately went wide. Lowry gave her a big wink and put a finger to his lips as a "keep quiet" gesture, then turned to her. She reached out her hand to shake, but Lowry threw his arms wide and pulled her into a hug before she could stop him.

"Olivia Michaelson!" He boomed into her ear. "I can't tell you how glad I am to see you! I never thought you'd meet with me. I'm so glad we could put our heads together on this. We can do great things together, it's going to be incredible. We'll make something that will make our grandmothers proud."

Everything about him as a human was clearly dialed all the way to eleven. Jesus Christ. "To tell you the truth, Mr. Lowry, if I'd known it was you, I wouldn't have come. I respect you as an artist, but I don't think Small and Sparkling's stories are going to particularly benefit from the attention of 'Tittybro.'"

She set her tone for 'absolutely scathing,' but it didn't seem to make a dent in his enthusiasm. "Oh, is that all you're worried about? I was worried that it was going to be the dragons. Those, I was absolutely responsible for, and I'm ashamed of them. They looked like whiskered rats with Play-Doh wings. I cut art department hours, and I got shitty art. I deserved it. But the titties, those make perfect sense. I can explain them. The bro thing, that was the internet, but it seems like everyone gets called some kind of bro these days. Anyway! Let's sit down and get to work."

She truly meant to walk away and find somewhere else to eat, but when he pulled out her chair, it was like years of social conditioning took over and the only solution was to sit down.

"I'm not sure my grandmother is ever going to be proud about someone flashing their chest around all the time." Olivia was shocked at how prudish she sounded, but this man was under her skin like a hair.

"Mine either," he said. "Mine smacked me on the arm last time I was home, told me that even whores didn't walk around naked so much, and to let a woman put a damn shirt on. But the thing is, all the boobs were so much better than what the network wanted. You see, they wanted nothing but sex. Blowjobs and rutting and doggie style and every other way they could think of to show off the actors they'd paid for. But the thing is, when you've got sex on the screen, that's all anybody sees. So, they wanted to cut all these plotlines to make room for the sex. But I loved those books as a kid, and I would have done anything to keep them as faithful an adaptation as possible. So, boobs. I pointed out that you could put boobs in just about any scene, just have a lady walking around topless. Lots of people like boobs and will keep their eyes on the screen just to watch 'em, even if the boobs are just kind of staying still. The network got their sex appeal, and I got to have the characters plot and scheme and keep the damn story going." He shrugged, grinning, and Olivia could almost see a cigar hanging out of the corner of his mouth. "Now I get called Tittybro on the internet. But, hey, I've been called worse things."

"And now you want to make your grandmother proud?" The conversation was moving faster than she could keep up with.

"Or at least stop smacking me. I'll take either one. Listen, let me ask, did you watch soaps with your grandma as a kid?" He was leaning over the table, eager and engaged. He had not gotten quieter even though they were just a few feet apart now.

"I...what?"

"See, growing up, my grandma watched me during the summers when my parents were working. And whatever we did, no matter what was happening, whether she was taking me to Bingo or the park or whatever else, we were home at 12:30 on the dot so she could watch her soapies. That's what she called them, her soapies. My mother called them 'Mom's stories,' but that was a little rude, you know? I loved them. They were ridiculous, bigger than life, people with millions of dollars and big dramatic lives but they were still running into everyday problems, like loving someone who didn't love them back. Well, you don't encounter evil twins every day. Although there was this one movie I worked on—"

He paused, shook his head, and grinned, clearly enjoying the memory but delightfully not sharing it. "Doesn't matter. The point is, she loved them, and she arranged her entire life to watch them every day. Even though you could watch most soaps two days a week and still know everything that's going on."

"Mr. Lowry—"

"Just a minute. What's good here?"

The rapid leap from topic to topic was making it hard for her to keep track of the conversation. It took her a minute to figure out what he was talking about now. "Oh. I was going to have the chicken parmesan."

He clapped his hands together so loudly that Olivia jumped, but Lowry was already onto the next thing, flagging down a waiter who hadn't come to their table yet. "Two chicken parms," he said. "And salads for sides—" he glanced back at Olivia, "Okay?" She nodded, unsure if it would make a difference. "Great, thanks." Another bill flashed out of his hand and into the waiter's. The waiter pocketed it more smoothly than the hostess had and nodded at them, assuring them that their food would be out soon.

"So did you do that?" He asked.

Olivia was getting tired of being behind in the conversation. "Watch soaps with my grandmother? Yes, I guess—"

He clapped his hands together and laughed loudly enough that people at other tables glanced over. "I knew it. I knew that no one would love romance as much as you and not have loved soaps as a kid. Tell me, do you still watch them?"

"I...no, I don't have time, and they're on during the middle of the day. Besides, for me, it was—"

"Exactly!" he said, cutting her off before she could explain about Jane Austen. "And prime time soaps are something completely different, and prestige dramas have killed them off anyway—gotta own that one, I fucking hate that it's my fault, but here we are—so there's nothing left to fill that gap. And we need it filled. At the risk of sounding like a porn star myself, there's gotta be something to fill that hole."

He paused and watched Olivia carefully, but if she was supposed to fill the hole in the conversation, she had no idea how.

"That's where you come in," he said, like she was very slow on the uptake. Which she currently was, to be fair. "You have the IPs—the property rights—and I have money to burn and a strong desire to have an online nickname that doesn't have the word 'titties' in it. Because, as stated, I like a good titty as much as the next straight allosexual guy, but I'm tired of my grandma smacking me, especially because I deserve it." He grinned. "In retrospect, I can admit that once the internet got ahold of it, it became a game around the office. How many titties could we fit in any episode. Guest star titties, background—"

"I swear, if you say titties one more time, you're going to get my water glass in your face." Somehow, she was smiling with exasperation instead of actually throwing something at him. The man had charisma for days. In another world, one where she wasn't missing a certain computer nerd so badly it hurt, it would have caught her attention.

"Boobs," he said, smoothly switching gears and wearing that cigar dangling grin again. "The point is, I'm not kidding. I want to make something my grandma can watch and still show her face at the senior center. You've got the stories, and I can make them sing. If you look at Asian dramas, they're huge online, and Americans who are willing to put up with subtitles love them, so if we give them the same idea, but with no reading required? They'll eat it up."

It sounded like hope, and Olivia had absolutely no room for that in her life right now. "And where's the money in it? Prestige dramas have killed off the primetime dramas, and blockbusters have killed romantic comedies, so why is anyone going to make sweet, dramatic little romantic soap operas? What network is going to care?"

"No network," he said. "But the internet will. And as for the money, there isn't any in it." He seemed to catch the meaning of her sharp gaze and waved it away. "There's not the kind of money that gets the attention of someone who financed a drama that got internet famous for naked breasts," his emphasis on the word was not rude, but he clearly meant for the word to be high- lighted. "But for the guy who wants to make his grandma happy? I can make sure that it breaks even, at least. And that your authors are well compensated."

Olivia studied Evan Lowry for a long time. "You mean every word you say, don't you?" The man seemed to be made entirely of ceramic veneers and loud clothing, but there was a sincerity to him that was startling.

"Of course," he said, looking honestly offended.

"Are you going to tell me that we'll make magic together?"

He rested his chin in his hand and gave her a smile that would have made the hearts of a dozen background actors drop their tops. "Will it work if I do?"

Maybe hope wasn't such an awful thing after all. "I don't know. Why don't you tell me more?" She had no idea if any of this was going to be worth anything at all—but it wouldn't hurt to listen. After all, the chicken parmesan was incredible.

Chapter 20

Thomas

Thomas's heart had been slamming when he got on the plane back to DC, and it felt like it was going to break his ribs now, as he walked up to the Italian restaurant where Olivia's calendar indicated that she was eating dinner with "Tits & Ass," whatever that meant. He was mildly ashamed that he'd checked her calendar to find out where she was, but not so ashamed he hadn't been willing to do it.

He hadn't meant to get on the plane. He'd had every plan in the world to figure out a way to work remotely, to commute out to the city for interviews, to travel back and forth if he needed to, if he found a job that required it, but when he came downstairs one afternoon, he found his father sitting in a chair with Thomas's tablet in his hand, the one where he'd been running various beta builds of the app he'd been building for S&S.

"You make this?" His dad had waved the tablet in the air without looking up from it. After a moment of silence, his father set down the tablet and looked at his son. "Obviously not the tablet, don't look at me like that, I'm not stupid."

Thomas winced. One thing lost to the stroke had been his father's filters. Thomas had always thought of his father as a straight-forward man who didn't hold much back, but it turned out there was a lot that he hadn't said after all. "I know you're not, Dad."

His father nodded and made a sort of 'glad that's settled' sound. "But the—what's it called? The..." He waved his hand in the air. Thomas kept quiet. The therapist had said that, at least for now, it was better to let his father work to find the words he'd forgotten unless he specifically asked for help. "The picture. Program. No. What is it?"

"App, short for application. And yes, I did make it."

"You write all these stories?"

Thomas laughed. "No. No, I'm good at code, not at real-life syntax." If he was good at real-life syntax, he would have found the words to explain to Olivia why everything was turning out the way it was.

"They're good. I like 'em better than the TV. They don't make my head hurt."

The moving pictures were turning out to be a problem. The therapist said that might improve, but it might not. Dad was definitely missing his nightly dose of whatever crime drama was on that night. Thomas would not have anticipated him picking romance serial stories instead.

"I'm glad," he said. "You can keep that, if you want."

"It's not done, though." His father pointed at a button on the screen. "When I tap that, nothing happens. I just get an error."

A thousand tech support agents screamed 'an error is something happening' in Thomas's head, and he fought them back. "It's not live," Thomas said. "So you can read the stories, but they're only based on a database backup. It's not connected to the network."

"Shame. I'd like to tell this lady that her stories were good." His dad smiled and waggled his eyebrows. "Specially the steamy bits."

"God, Dad!" Sometimes it didn't take much to turn you into a grossed out pre-teen. This was one of those things.

His dad shrugged. "Sometimes a person gets lonely. I figure you know that, since you've been up nights talking to someone. Sounds like a girl, from what I can hear. I know you have to be careful just saying that these days, because you can't tell just from someone sounds, so I'm sorry if I've got that wrong."

"She is a woman," Thomas said. "Olivia. She's who I was working for. That app was for her company."

"Was?"

"I'm going to quit. I can't do the job I was hired to do properly from here."

His dad's brow furrowed. "Where are you planning to go, if not back to the city?"

"Here," he said. "You need me."

His dad scoffed and waved his hand in the air. His left hand, because his right hand wasn't good for much detail work these days. The therapist seemed less optimistic about him getting that back, but she said 'you never know what physical therapy can do, especially if he's willing to work hard.' "The girls have this handled."

"That's not fair to them." Thomas tried to make it sound like something he believed, but it didn't quite work. It wasn't fair to them, but what could he really do here? Other than stand around and be in the way.

His dad waved that away as well. "You're just going to be in the way here. I don't mean that to be unkind, but you've never been happy in this town. Not since you were a kid, and certainly not after your mom passed. You can't make this," he waved the tablet in the air, "here."

"The nice thing about remote work—"

"If it was really nice, you wouldn't be quitting your job," his dad interrupted. "Did Abby put you up to this?"

"What? No."

"You're a bad liar, Thomas. She lays on a guilt trip like your mother. She's already explained to me twice about how I'm going to work extra hard at physical therapy or else I'll be letting down my future grandchildren or something."

"She's not wrong."

"Don't you start. The point is that...if she's trying to get you to stay here, then she's not doing what's right." His dad was quiet for a long minute, and when he spoke, his voice was quiet. This voice was a distant memory, one he'd only heard in the years before his mom died. The memory was faded and worn, but it felt warm. "I'd love to have my son nearby. But not if he's unhappy."

"I'm not—"

"You're a bad liar, don't try me."

Thomas couldn't bring himself to say more. But then, his silence had spoken plenty.

"You like that woman? The one you've been talking to?"

"Yes."

"Then go back to your damn big city and stop worrying about your sister. She's only happy when she's got someone to boss around, but it doesn't need to be you. Trust me, I'll be taking up most of her time for the next while." There was sadness around his father's eyes. The man was too hard to admit weakness now, but he knew what had happened and what he was facing. He was daunted by it, if not outright afraid. "You just come back and visit sometimes. More than you do. She'll settle down, and I won't have to miss my son so much."

That last thing was said to the ceiling, which was fine, because there was far too much emotion in the air for Thomas to look directly at his father either.

"And I'm keeping this," his father said, waving the tablet around again. "You let me know when that app is finished so I can download it. I want to tell that woman about how good her story is."

"I'll send you a better tablet," Thomas said. "A bigger one. Easier to use."

"Sure," his father said. "That'd be okay."

And Thomas had left the room and started to pack. Put a ticket back to the city on Mason's credit card, texted Mason to let him know and apologize, and checked Olivia's calendar. He'd gotten an Uber directly from the airport to the restaurant. And now, looking in the window, he could see her sitting at a table with a man. She was facing him, but clearly not seeing him, because the man she was with was holding her hand and...pressing his lips to it? Thomas did not normally think of himself as a jealous man, but what tore through him in that moment was nothing more than the purest rage at seeing someone else touch what was clearly his. He had slammed the door open before he knew what was happening, started the hostess enough that he moved right past her, and stormed up to the table.

"What the hell," he said, his voice louder than he meant it to be and completely incredulous. "What are you doing here? What's all this?"

He sounded like the biggest douche on the planet, and he tried to get himself under control, but there was something in him on the edge of breaking. He'd listened to his father, he'd pissed off his sister—Abby had left him three voicemails and he hadn't listened to any of them—and he'd...done nothing but disappoint the most beautiful woman he'd ever known over and over again. His bravado faded, and shame flooded into the spaces it had filled. Of course she had someone else kissing her hand. He hadn't been there to do it, and she deserved someone who would.

Olivia was looking at him with complete horror, her hand still in the man's. The man had turned to look at him, and Thomas thought for a moment that the guy looked familiar somehow, but it was a big city; everyone started to look vaguely familiar before long. "Thomas," Olivia said, her voice steadier than his had been, but not by much. "I...you didn't say you were coming back."

"I didn't know I needed to," he said, although that was obviously a lie. He'd done nothing to make it clear to her that he was coming back, that he would be there for her no matter what. Hell, it wasn't true. Just that morning, he'd been writing a resignation letter and trying to figure out how to tell her that he wouldn't, couldn't, be back. Jesus, he was a fucking idiot. "Look, I'm sorry. I'm going to—you two enjoy yourself. Olivia, I'll come by the office and collect my things on Monday, I'm sorry."

The man had dropped Olivia's hand by now. He looked back and forth between Olivia and Thomas, then let out a huge sigh and stood. Thomas prepared himself for the punch to the jaw, ready to try and shift so he could take it on the shoulder and not end up with a broken bone on top of whatever was squeezing the shit out of his heart. Instead, the guy stretched out his hand to shake.

"Hi," he said. "Sorry to give you the wrong idea. I'm 'Tittybro.'"

Complete silence reined for several seconds. Thomas's mind was completely blank as he tried frantically to understand what the shit was happening. Then it started to click. Tittybro. That dude on the internet who made the shows with all the fucking. Who had wanted to talk to Olivia about the stories at S&S. Oh, shit. This was a ... oh *shit*.

"Oh...wow. Shit. I'm..." There were no words to make up for this. He stuck his hand out and shook the guy's —something Jacobs? No, Lowry—and tried to think of something to say that wouldn't make him a complete asshole and ruin Olivia's chances at whatever the hell was happening here.

"Don't worry about it," Lowry said. "Frankly, I'm flattered that I look like I can hook a woman as good-looking and intelligent as your friend Olivia here." He stressed the word friend, made it into a question.

"More than friend," Thomas said, doing his best to meet Olivia's gaze and hope that she wouldn't personally throw him into the sun for leaping in here like a jealous tomcat pissing on the walls. "At least, I hope she still is."

"Let's go talk about it," Olivia said. "We'd just finished eating. Evan—I'd say I'll have my people call your people, but my people are me, so..."

He nodded. "You have my number, and I'll be waiting for your call. Have a great afternoon. And a great night.

And a great morning. Whatever you two crazy kids get up to." He waggled his eyebrows like he was Groucho Marx. "Put on one of my shows, if it gets your engine's cranky. I didn't earn the name Tittybro for nothing."

Olivia raised one eyebrow in a haughty expression. "What would your grandmother think of that?"

Lowry burst out laughing. Olivia stood up and Thomas took her hand, squeezing it tight. He couldn't remember, suddenly, if he'd actually just held her hand like this before. It felt like one of the most right things that had ever occurred in the universe. "I can't wait to make more of her 'stories' with you, Olivia. Thanks for taking my meeting."

She nodded, and Thomas took the opportunity to pull her close, heading out of the restaurant before she could be distracted with more small talk. He needed to talk to her, and he needed her alone.

Outside the restaurant, Thomas pulled her into a close hug. "I'm sorry for being an Alpha hole," he said.

She leaned back, grinning. "When did you pick up that particular term?"

He shrugged. "There were a lot of hours in the hospital with Dad, and S&S has an incredible back catalogue. Figured I should research the product more. In fact, that's part of what I want to talk to you about. Can I take you out for coffee?"

Olivia studied him like he was a painting in a museum. "No," she said, eventually.

His heart tumbled down into his shoes. "No?"

"No. There's much better coffee at my place."

The rapid ascent of his heart almost made him dizzy. "Are you—"

"Don't ask me silly questions," she said. "I've been missing you every second since you left. You took off for a completely understandable reason, and I will never ever resent you for that, but you left me with a hell of a problem." She ducked her head a little, something he'd never seen her do, and looked up at him through her pretty, perfectly made-up eyelashes. "I've been trying to fix it with my vibrator, but I think I've burned out the motor. I think I just need a...hands on approach." She pulled him closer, wrapping her arms around the small of her back. "Think you can give me that?"

It took an amazing amount of willpower to make sure his cock wasn't painfully hard; he still had to walk to wherever her car was and wait while she drove home. The fact that there was almost certainly a blind alley within walking distance was no excuse for the filthy thoughts flooding into his brain. She deserved better.

At least, the first time.

"Yes, Liv." Using the nickname while looking into her eyes made everything in him sing. "Yes, I'm sure I can."

She threaded her fingers through his again. "Then let's go."

Chapter 21

Olivia

As she and Thomas walked to her car—much faster than she might have bothered to walk on other days, notably—her phone rang. Olivia was tempted to send the call directly to voicemail, but when she saw her sister's name on the caller ID, she gave Thomas an apologetic look. "I'm really sorry," she said. "Give me a couple minutes."

Thomas nodded and stepped a few feet away to let her at least pretend she was in a private space. She stepped under a tree and picked up the call. "Lydia? Honey, it's not the best—" The sound of her sister's tears stunned her into silence. Lydia never cried.

"I've had enough," Lydia said through her sobs. "I'm leaving him."

It took a moment for Olivia to put it together, and another to squash the little cry of delight in her heart. Lydia's husband, Tristan, had never been one of her favorite people. She'd kept it to herself since the day she started dating, and now was not the time for "I told you so," but if Lydia was actually done, Olivia was certainly not going to suggest that her sister try and make the relationship work. "Lydia, what's going on?"

Thomas was looking at her curiously and she gave him a little shrug. On the phone, Lydia took a deep, shuddering breath.

"They offered me junior partner," she said. "At the firm."

Olivia let out a little squeal of joy. Her genius little sister had been working so hard for so long to make this work. And then she put it together. "I'm so glad for you, that's fantastic," she said. "I'm guessing it didn't go as well at home?"

Lydia laughed, but there was nothing funny to say the least. "No. No, it did not go well. Tristan...he said some shit. Some...I'm not dealing with this anymore. It's enough."

"Can you tell me what's going on?"

Lydia sighed. "It's such a long story, Liv. It's one of those things...it didn't start today. Clearly. I mean, it never does."

"Are you talking to lawyers?"

"Yeah. And mine says I have to stay in the condo while we"re separated because otherwise it's leaving the family home and can work against me or something. Though honestly, he's making noise like he might leave to just make this easier. I don't know." She sighed, long and deep. "Can I come visit you? We can do mani-pedis and go on stupid drinking binges."

"Yeah, of course. Absolutely. Anything you need."

Lydia made a little gulping sound; she was clearly choking back tears. "I'm at work right now. I just needed a break. Can I call you tonight?"

Olivia eyed Thomas and briefly weighed how much she wanted to take care of her sister with how much she needed this man in every way she could to have him.

Her little sister seemed to read her mind. "How are things going with your 'assistant'?" she asked, making the word sound completely lascivious.

Olivia felt a flush spread up her cheeks. "I think things are about to take a turn for the really, really good."

"The really, really sexy?"

The flush might light her on fire if she wasn't careful. "It's probable."

Lydia laughed. "Call me tomorrow then. Or the day after. You pick."

"Honey, no—"

"Olivia. Please listen to me and believe me right now. Nothing in the entire world will make me feel happier than knowing my stuffy, obnoxiously perfect, sister is getting some. A lot. I would say 'enjoy some for me' but I'm pretty sure that's way creepy."

Ew. "I would agree."

"Then please. Enjoy yourself. I promise, I'm a fuck-ing mess, but given the potential messiness of a fucking mess, I'm doing okay." The huge, snotty sniff gave lie to the statement, but Olivia decided to trust.

"Okay. You'll call me if that changes? I'll be here in a second if you need me. You know that?"

"Of course. Stop being ridiculous. Go have some lunchtime nookie." Some of the sadness seemed to have leaked out of Lydia's voice. "My big sister, finally living life on the edge."

"It's not like that..."

"Of course it is, and it's about time it is." There was a huge honk as Lydia blew her nose with absolutely no grace at all. "I love you. I'll talk to you soon. Have fun."

The phone went silent as Lydia hung up. Olivia stared at the dark screen for a long moment, trying to will it back into lighting up and making some sense. "Why did she even call me?" she asked the air.

"Who was it?" Thomas had walked closer to her now that the call had clearly been disconnected.

"My sister," Olivia said. "I don't...maybe she's getting divorced? She hung up pretty fast."

"Do you want to call her back?"

She looked Thomas up and down, not trying to hide her interest. Not trying to pretend that she was cool. Put together. Professional. Worried about the fact that she was ten years older than him. "If it were really urgent, she would have told me so. I think she just...needed to shout that at someone? I don't know."

"Sisters," Thomas said, his voice both cryptic and sympathetic.

"Agreed," Olivia said. She needed to get Lydia thoroughly out of her head. There was one very easy way to do that. She took a step forward, wrapped her arms around Thomas's neck, and kissed him as thoroughly as she knew how. He responded in a heartbeat, pulling her tight against him and making a soft sound into her mouth. And then a less soft sound.

"I love kissing you, Liv, I really do. But we should definitely not be in public right now. I think we should be somewhere very, very private." His hand pressed at the small of her back, snugging her up tight against him and making it very clear just how private he wanted them to be. She could feel him, and more than that, she could remember how it had felt when he had held her, his mouth on her, how he'd made her scream.

"Yes," she said, and it was all she needed to say.

They made it back to her house in record time. Thomas's mouth was on her neck as she struggled with her keys to get the door open; as soon as they were inside, he kicked the door shut and shoved her up against the wall. She cursed the stupid decision she'd made that morning to put on pants; without them, she was sure that he would already have his hands on her body.

He tore his mouth away from her long enough to pull his t-shirt up over his head, tossing it in the corner. She got her blouse untucked and fumbled with the buttons. It was half off before he was kissing her again, his mouth wild over her, kissing and licking at his skin with total abandon.

"Bed," she said. "I want you in my bed. Now."

He laughed against her neck. "Look who's getting bossy now," he said. "Do you think you should get to order me around, beautiful?" He pulled her tight against him again. "I don't take orders well, I'm not going to lie. But I do take requests."

Her cheeks flushed bright red. "Fine. Thomas, I would like to formally request that you fuck me until I'm screaming your name. How's that sound?"

He groaned, grinding on her for just a moment as he bit at her neck. His fingers were teasing at her nipples and she whimpered, soaking wet already and hungry for him. She was vaguely aware of how thick he was, how nervous she'd been about taking him, but right now, she couldn't make herself care.

"Conveniently," he said, "That is in line with what I had in mind, so yes, I'm happy to oblige you on that." He stepped back enough to let her move past him down the hallway and gave her ass a swat as she went past. She turned to shoot an offended look at him, and he laughed. "Move faster."

She did.

Time seemed to slow down when they made it into the bedroom. Or maybe it was just them. Something seemed to go soft in the air. Thomas's hands were shaking as he undid the last few buttons from her shirt and slipped it off her shoulders. He kissed his way down her skin to her breasts, unfastening her bra and letting the heavy weight fall into his hands. He teased her nipples with his teeth while she sighed happily against him. In this very moment, she couldn't remember how many times he'd made her come, but she wasn't entirely sure he'd seen her topless before. And then she flushed with nervousness. Had he ever seen her really, all the way naked? She wasn't sure she had. Self-consciousness made her cross her arms over her belly and lean away from him just a little.

"Hey," he said, slowing down and giving her space. "What's happening, beautiful?"

"Are you sure you want this?" It was the only way she could think to ask for reassurance without blatantly saying that she was worried he wouldn't find her attractive.

He didn't respond with words. He ran his hands over her, tracing her neck and the sides of her breasts with his fingertips, trailing his hands down her waist and gripping her full ass in his hands. He followed his fingers with kisses, making her shiver and whimper as he traced over her nipples again. He tugged the left one taut with his finger as he pressed his mouth against hers again. "Yes," he said, twisting hard enough to make her whimper. "I promise."

"Then take me," she said. It was the most Jane Austen line she'd ever spoken in her life, and she was proud of it, somehow.

"I'm not sure I could stop myself," he said. Between them, they shed her pants and then his. He was shockingly gorgeous, as thick and heavy as she'd imagined. He moved her toward the bed, but she shook her head.

"Not yet," she said, and dropped to her knees.

"Liv, fuck." He groaned when she took his cock in her hand, and he cursed when she kissed the tip. She sized him up. She'd never even tried to take someone this thick in her mouth, but the thought of trying...mmm. She opened as wide as she could and wrapped her mouth around him, holding him steady as she pressed forward.

He cursed again, one hand on the back of her head to steady himself. She could feel his hips shivering with the need to push himself forward, make her take him. She almost wanted him to. She pulled back and then sucked him deeper, maybe halfway down his shaft. His hand tightened in her hair, guiding her motions, not forcing her but letting her see how he wanted it. She managed to take a little more of him with every stroke, not all of him but enough that she could press her lips against where her fingers were holding him steady. He shivered against her, his hand trembling. She could feel him on the edge of losing control, holding himself steady, so close to the edge that she had just a minute to decide whether she was going to try and swallow him--

He yanked back from her, gasping for air. "Next time," he said. "Holy shit. Your mouth is incredible. But next time."

"Next time?" She quirked an eyebrow at him.

"Give me your phone," he said.

"Um. What?"

"Your phone. Where is it."

"In my purse, probably. Which I think is still somewhere in the kitchen."

"Great." He grabbed his pants off the floor and pulled his phone out of the pocket. "Hold on."

Buck naked, he walked out of the room. She heard a couple of beeps, and then the fridge door opened and closed. He came back, looking ridiculously proud of himself. "Did you...juts put your phone in my refrigerator?"

"And yours," he said. "I don't have a Faraday cage handy, but I figure it'll do. I am absolutely not going to be interrupted again." He stroked his cock lightly, just enough to keep her eyes focused on him as he drank her in, studying her like he was memorizing her. "I'm planning to fuck you until we're both exhausted, Liv. Olivia. Until you want me to stop. Because I've been waiting too long for this."

"And what if I don't want you to stop?"

He got close to her, pulled her into his arms, and kissed her like the romantic hero in all of her dreams. "Then I never will," he said. He pressed a light kiss on her forehead, then gently pushed. She fell back onto the bed willingly enough.

He knelt between her thighs, kissing his way down the inside of one and then the other—then paused. "Shit. I should have asked. Do you have condoms?"

"Don't need them unless you want them," Olivia said. "I'm on the pill and I got tested not too long ago."

"Also tested. And...god, I love that I get to fuck you bare."

He leaned forward, kissing her as his fingers pressed between her thighs, exploring her pussy and spreading that wetness until she was slick with it. She was hungry for him, her body arching and seeking him. "Stop wasting time," she said, kissing him as hard as she could, nipping at his lip and loving the cruel little sound he made. "I want you inside me."

"I'm not trying to be arrogant," he said. "But I don't want to hurt you."

She laughed. "I'm a big girl," she said. "I can take it."

That won her a big smile. "You live to test my self-control."

"Next time," she said, running her hand down his cheek. "Go slow next time. Now? I want you to fuck me."

He pushed two thick fingers into her without saying anything else. She cried out, arching against his fingers. Jesus, she was a little tight around them, how was she possibly going to take that thick cock. "I'll get to it," he said, rocking his fingers into her as she met him, thrust for thrust. "Let me take care of you."

He curled his fingers, moving so that her movements sent his fingers dragging over something heated deep in her body, leaving her gasping. When he pressed his thumb onto her clit, catching her on both sides and stroking her, she swore. "Fuck, Thomas. I want to come on you. I want your goddamn cock."

"Get a lady a little heated and she swears like a sailor," he teased, his fingers not slowing at all. She felt him press a third finger inside, and she was so full she ached, how was she possibly going to take him-- "Trust me, beautiful," he said. "Trust me and let go."

The words were somehow enough. With no warning, she felt herself shatter, her body tightening around him so hard that she saw stars. Her back arched, and waves of pleasure tore through her.

Before her body had fully worn out the pleasure he was there, his thick cock pressing into her. She cried out at heat of him, the size of him. Her body was soft and eager and hungry, and he still had to push his way in. He went slowly, steady little thrusts that took him deeper and deeper, utterly unrelenting. It somehow dragged out the orgasm, kept the pleasure shifting in little waves, and with each surge of her body, he slipped forward a little more until he bottomed out in her, their bodies fully seated together. She wanted to cry at how incredibly good it felt. How much it hurt. How much she didn't care.

"You okay?" he asked, his voice careful.

Her voice trembled. "Thomas. If you don't fuck me right now, I'll do something really unpleasant that I will absolutely be able to think about when I'm not...begging you to fuck me. Please. I've waited so long. I want to feel you." She caught his gaze and held it. "Please fuck me."

Chapter 22

Thomas

What the hell was a guy supposed to say when he was balls-deep in a gorgeous woman who'd just asked him to fuck her? Your wish is my command? Yes ma'am? He filed 'okay, boss' away for a day when she might not be so insecure.

He didn't bother with the words. A picture was worth a thousand, right, so how much was one stroke of his cock worth? Based on the look on her face, plenty, because that one push and pull had her back arching, had her whispering oh god oh god so soft that he wasn't even sure she could hear him.

He wanted to go slow, desperately wanted to go slow and make this incredible for her, but his body clearly had other plans. He was aching, he'd been desperate for relief in her for so long, and he was finally here. Feeling her soft and sweet and so painfully tight around him that he'd almost had to force himself into her when she was still surging from that orgasm.

He tried to go slow, but Liv had other plans. She caught the back of his neck, pulled him down to kiss him so hard that their teeth clacked together, and got one leg wrapped around his waist, pulling him tighter even though she clearly felt the sting even harder. "I said fuck me," she said.

He couldn't control himself. No, that wasn't true. He just didn't want to. He slammed into her, hard, and when she let out a little whimper, he stroked her cheek. "Oh, none of that, beautiful," he said. "You know you can take this."

Her hands dug into his ass, pulling him hard, and he stopped even pretending to hold back. He surged into her, feeling her pulse tight around him as she met him, stroke for stroke. He hadn't been teasing her before, it had taken everything he had not to come in her mouth, and he was already dancing on the edge. He thought about slowing down, taking his time—but no. No. There would be more times. More chances. They'd agreed. He had to believe she wanted it.

He let his body take over, let him drive into her as hard as he wanted to, not paying attention to her little whimpers and cries, trusting that she would tell him if it was too much, trusting that she would share with him, trusting that she would trust him.

"You feel so good," she murmured, and it was enough. His body went wild for another half dozen strokes, slamming her so hard that he thought the bed might break, and then the orgasm tore him apart. He let out a loud cry that was half her name and half a thank you to whatever gods might be paying attention because of how incredible she felt. How she pulled him down to him, stroking his back as he thrust into her a last few times, his pleasure playing itself out as he tried to catch his ragged breath.

"I love you," he said. And then he froze, shocked that the words had come out of his mouth. He'd started thinking them a while ago, longer ago than he wanted to admit, but he'd never even considered saying them out loud. His mind went into a panic spiral, worried about what she'd think or say, she was so careful, so cautious, what if it was too soon--

"I love you too," she said, her soft caresses on his back never slowing.

He leaned back, lifting himself up just enough that he could look into her eyes.

"What?" She shrugged. "You said it first. By every law in every romance that's ever existed, I'm allowed to say it back." Her eyes were teasing. "I'm a modern woman, I could have said it first if I wanted to. But now I don't have to wait." She leaned up and kissed him. "I love you."

"I'm so incredibly lucky," he said.

"It's true," she replied, her eyes teasing and sincere at the same time. "And so am I."

Chapter 23

Olivia

She lost track of how many times she came that night, or how many times he did. If she tried to list the different positions they'd found, she'd have needed a pad of paper, a pen, and some time to think. It was corny cliché nonsense, but she really never had felt the way Thomas made her feel. Precious and cherished and loved. Yes, loved.

Eventually, they were sweaty and tired and sated, at least for the moment. They took a shower together, and he had her one more time up against the wall, fingering her until she came on his cock, then following her over the edge like a tidal wave. Then they curled up in bed, wrapped around each other, his fingers tight in hers. They dozed for a little bit.

When Olivia woke up, her head was a little clearer. Thomas was still half asleep, his eyelashes resting on his cheeks. She shifted a little closer to him, but it was just enough movement that his eyes opened. "Hey, beauti-ful," he said, pressing a soft kiss against her lips. It was a sign of how tired they both were that he didn't immedi-ately stir against her hip, and she was not immediately soaked. "How're you feeling?"

"Sore," she said, laughing. "And so good."

"Good." He snuggled her closer, his face buried in her neck. "You smell nice."

She laughed and swatted his shoulder lightly. "You're the one who told me which shower gel to use."

"I picked well. What can I say, I have excellent taste."

She drifted with him for a few minutes, just luxuri-ating in the sensation of a man who loved her holding her close. Something she wasn't sure she'd ever felt—not like this, at least. And then her brain clicked over to something that had seemed wildly unimportant at the time. "You wanted to show me something."

He laughed. "I showed you a lot of things. I have more things I'm happy to show you, but I think you should get a rest first. Maybe be a little less sore."

"Not that," she said. "When you were at the restau-rant. You said you had something to show me."

That made him go still. "Ah. That."

She shifted up onto her elbows so she could look at him. "Something wrong?"

"No," he said. "Just self-conscious, that's all."

She sat up, taking a long look up and down his body. He was bare naked, his arms crossed behind his head, eyeing her. "I'm not sure what you have to be self-conscious about."

He laughed. "Maybe you only like me for my body."

She swatted at him, and he caught her hand easily. "What did you want to show me?"

He pulled her down into a kiss. "I know you said it wouldn't make a difference." He planted a light kiss on her lips, then looked at her seriously. "But once I started working on it, I wanted to see it through. Even if you decide it's worthless. I wanted you to see what it could look like."

"So, show me."

He sighed. She couldn't laugh at him, but he looked more nervous now than he had when he stripped down in front of her, and far more nervous than he had when he'd gone and practically challenged a stranger to a duel for her honor. "Wait here," he said. He pulled on his pants as he stepped out of the bedroom. What was that song? She was sad to watch him go, but Lord, to watch him leave. She enjoyed an eyeful of his gorgeous ass, and when he was out of sight, she grabbed a clean t-shirt and pajama shorts out of her bureau. When he came back, she was sitting on the bed, her legs crossed. He sat down next to her, holding a tablet. He turned the screen on, then passed it to her.

"What--" The logo for Small and Sparkling filled the screen for a moment before opening to a carousel of book covers. "What is this?"

"It's not up to date," he said. "I built it off the backup of the site from right after I—had to leave."

"When did you have time?" Olivia scrolled through the covers on the screen. It looked like many of the serial fiction apps she'd seen, but when she tapped on a cover, there were options she hadn't seen before. Messaging the author. A comments section. Was that a way for someone to friend another user?

"I had nothing but time," he said. "I was waiting for appointments, waiting for doctors, waiting for rides, waiting for wheelchairs. Waiting for everything. If I hadn't had this to do, I would have invented something else to code. I coded sense into the world when everything was falling apart. That sounds corny, but it's true."

"It's poetic."

"Anyway," he said, brushing away the comment. "It's a little more than a wireframe, but it's at least a proof of concept. It would take...somewhere between 18 months and two years, probably, to get it up and running and really make it sing the way it could. I know you don't think much of it, but I swear—even my father liked it. I found him reading a bunch of stories one night. Said I should tell some of the authors to get their stories updated and was pissed as hell when I told him that there were probably more updates that I couldn't get him until I got a laptop for him."

"Are you serious?"

"Of course." He was staring at her, which was fair. She would have been staring at herself about now. She was scrolling through the screens faster, finding a million improvements she hadn't even known she had wanted in the other, similar apps she'd seen. Highlighting and bookmarking pages for later. Notifications not just for when an author posted a new chapter, but when they started a new story. A way for authors to link out to their own socials or a newsletter. She probably looked like a—well, like a woman who was starting to think there might be a light at the end of the tunnel. "What's going on?"

"You think this could be ready in 18 months?"

Thomas went quiet for a long moment. He stared off into the middle distance, muttering to himself a little. When she glanced at his hands, she could see his fingers twitching just a little, like he was tapping on a keyboard she couldn't see. "Definitely within two years. If I had the right team, and we could hit the ground running, then yes. 18 months. We could be ready for beta in about 15 months and a full launch in 18." He blinked, his vision clearing as he came back to her. "Why? What are you thinking?"

She tossed the tablet to the side, put her hands on both of his cheeks, and kissed him as fiercely as she possibly could. "I think you're the missing piece," she said. She stroked a finger down his cheek as he smiled. "I think you're exactly what I need. I think this might be perfect."

"I'm glad," he said. He reached to pull her down, his hands already roaming, but she pushed back.

"I need five minutes," she said. "I have to send a text."

He raised his eyebrows and she laughed.

"I promise! I'll put my phone right back in the fridge when I'm done. I just...need to take care of this."

"Who are you texting?"

"Your roommate. To tell him that I do want his cash after all. I have a plan."

To his credit, Thomas didn't waste his time asking her about the plan. It didn't matter right now. What mattered was his hands all over her body, making her feel things she never dreamed she could.

***

A week later, the plan that had seemed like a stroke of absolute genius when she was fuck drunk and delirious on admitting love in her bedroom was making her palms sweat. Olivia paced in her office, shaking her hands out to keep from wiping her palms on her neatly pressed grey slacks. She doubted they would leave marks, but why risk it?

Thomas reached out and snagged one of her hands, pulling her close to him. He stroked her hair back from her face and kissed her temple. "It's going to be fine."

"Yes. You're right. It will be. But what if it isn't?"

"No point in worrying about it because it'll be fine," Thomas said. When she tried to argue again, he just kissed her. That was fine with her, honestly. She'd keep arguing all day long if it meant he kept kissing her to get her to stop. That was a plan she could work with.

She pulled back before she let herself get off track and thoroughly distracted both of them. "You sent your dad the laptop?"

He laughed and took her hands in his so she'd stop twisting them over each other. She let him and tried to focus on breathing. "Yes, Liv, I sent the laptop to my dad. I bookmarked all the pages he was looking for. I promised he could be one of our first beta testers. I even showed him how to get to Jenny Lawson's social media pages."

That was what today was about, really. Jenny Lawson. Keeping her with S&S. Everything hinged on that. Well, not technically; there were other authors who would take advantage of the opportunities Olivia was putting together if Jenny, quite reasonably, decided that she was done with S&S and was ready to move on. But Jenny had been one of her first authors. They'd worked together so closely at the beginning.

Everyone else had already agreed. This was the last piece that needed to fall into place for this puzzle to all fit together.

"She's going to say no."

Thomas didn't bother continuing to argue. Sometimes, it was her favorite thing about him. He seemed to know when she needed to just spin in a circle and be nervous and fretful until the worry passed and she could breathe again.

"How's your sister?" he asked.

Olivia blew out a breath. "As well as she can be," she said. "She and Tristan got married young, you know? And she was convinced it was love. But he's...I don't know. I'm glad they're getting a divorce. I'm sorry she's going through this. She's trying to be cheerful about all of it. But she's more down than I'd like."

"Is there anything you can do to help?"

"More than I'm doing? I don't know. She's got people all over the legal aspects, clearly, so I'm just sitting around and trying to big sister her to death. I sent her chocolate cake. It was her favorite as a kid. It seemed to make her smile." Olivia glanced at her watch again. "Is it too early to go to the conference room?"

Thomas sighed. "Will you feel better there?"

"No, but at least I'll stop worrying about tripping on a computer cord and breaking my neck walking to the room. One thing to cross off the list."

"Let's go then."

They stepped out of her office. Olivia gave a little wave to Samantha, the new assistant Thomas had hand-picked and was training. Now that they were dating, it seemed too tacky for him to be her assistant. Besides, there was other work that he was much more suited for. Even if he did joke constantly about how he'd always be her boy-toy, no matter what job he had.

Of course, given how much she kissed him when he said it, it was no wonder he kept making the joke.

She'd never thought it was going to be like this for her. As much as she'd dreamed of meeting her own romantic hero who would sweep her off her feet, this was better than any daydream she'd ever had.

Thomas followed her into the conference room. Most of the people she'd assembled were already in the room —Mason, Cassie, and now her and Thomas. Evan Lowry had conferenced into the call from LA. Olivia could see that he was on a call on his cellphone, his screen muted. He looked animated, gesturing and waving his hands around, laughing so hard he looked like he might fall out of his chair.

Thomas went and placed the call to Jenny, who was waiting by her computer as she'd said she would be. As Thomas got her up on the screen as well, Olivia sent a ping to Evan. He wrapped up his call and took himself off mute. "Sorry, everyone! Just got off a call with a fantastic actress, love her, she's looking for something to take in a new direction, project that'll knock her socks off. I told her I'd be calling her back in about half an hour with some excellent news, so hit me with it!"

That was, of course, the moment that Jenny's end of the call connected.

The two of them couldn't be less alike. Jenny had an air of busy-mom about her. Her hair was up in an off-kilter bun, not because it was artistic, but because she probably hadn't redone it since she tossed it up that morning. She hadn't put on any makeup, and her idea of business attire was putting on a plain t-shirt instead of one with a band logo. Her author photo was all wild hair and romantic gaze, but Olivia knew that Jenny had been wearing lounge pants along with that billowy blouse.

Olivia had never met anyone more put together who looked more like a walking train wreck.

"Evan Lowry, I presume," Jenny said.

"Jennifer Lawson!" he replied, his arms thrown wide. Was this man ever less than wildly boisterous? He seemed like the physical embodiment of 'Hollywood.' "The woman I want to make famous!" He leaned into the screen with a leer. "I showed my grandmother your stories, and she loves them, I have to tell you, she said some things about them that I told her, I never wanted to hear those words from her mouth again, and she said that with everything I've put on TV, she didn't ever want to hear me complain--"

"I'm so glad we could all get together today," Olivia said, loudly enough to cut Evan off, though his oversized grin was perfectly in place. Over the past week, she'd talked to him half a dozen times. He'd never stopped a sentence on his own. "Jenny, thanks for getting together with us. I know you've had some concerns about the direction that Small and Sparkling is taking, and whether this is going to be the right place for you to continue with your work."

"It's nothing personal, Olivia, I promise you."

"I understand," she said. And she really did. "But that's why I'm coming to you first. We're going to move in some new directions with S&S, and I hope you want to be a part of this new direction. You've always been the heart of this company's stories, Jenny. I don't want that to change."

"I'm listening." The woman was reserved, but she didn't look closed off. Just waiting. Olivia crossed her fingers below the table. Thomas had sat down on her left, and she felt his knee press against hers for just a moment, a tiny bit of comfort to calm her pounding heart.

"There's a lot of details that I'll explain as we go, but there are two key items. First, I want you to meet Thomas." She gestured to Thomas, who waved and nodded his head. "He's going to be in charge of developing a new mobile app for Small and Sparkling. We've talked about this before, and I know you've understood my reservations about bringing something to market unless we could distinguish ourselves in some ways."

Jenny nodded, not saying anything.

"Thomas has some exciting ideas about how to do exactly that. Increasing author engagement, offering tools to readers that the other apps just don't have. Your stories are the biggest and most comprehensive we have. Frankly, your fans have the potential to make or break this platform. I really hope you'll try it out with us."

Jenny opened her mouth, and the crease between her eyebrows told Olivia that she needed to talk fast.

"But that's not all," she said. Shit, she sounded like Bob Barker. Ugh. Well, she didn't have time to course correct, just time to keep going. "Mr. Lowry is here with us because he wants to help S&S do something really exciting."

Evan took himself off mute for just a moment. "Without tits."

Olivia was going to kill him. "Yes, something exciting with an absolute bare minimum of bare breasts. He wants to help us create a web TV platform that will adapt the IPs of our highest performing stories. Author participation won't just be a suggestion, it will be practically required. As much as the author wants. Direction, creative control, a voice at the table. And I will personally be making sure that those voices are heard."

Jenny was nodding along, but that note of careful reservation was in her voice. "These sound like exciting opportunities, Olivia, but the word on the street has been that the company is struggling. I'm sorry to be blunt. But frankly, on some of the author boards, people have been worried about whether or not we'll keep getting paid."

Olivia's stomach twisted. How had she let things get so far out of control? She could have wrecked everything with her stubbornness. But that was behind her now. Now, she was moving forward. Now, she had a plan. "I have an angel investor in place," she said, nodding to Mason. "He's willing to bankroll S&S as much as necessary for the next two years while we get the app up and running and Mr. Lowry starts seeing returns on his work. He is willing to agree to have no public involvement at S&S, just a promise that if I ever do sell, he'll see a return on his investment at that time. I know you're familiar with Cassie," another wave. "She'll be taking on the heading the new IP department of the company. Coordinating everything between the authors and Mr. Lowry's production company."

"And you want to start with my story?"

"Yes. It's the best one we have." Olivia took a long breath. "It's the best story we've ever had, Jenny. I hope you want to do this with us."

Olivia held her breath. That was her pitch. If Jenny passed, there were other authors she was sure would take the opportunity, but this was what she wanted. This was the keystone moment.

It seemed like a year before Jenny spoke. "I suspect I'm going to need an agent for this. Let's see what we need to do to get this started."

The cheer that went around the room was more than Olivia had ever dared to dream of.

Epilogue

One Year Later

"Get the popcorn!" Olivia shouted at Thomas. She was sitting on the couch, the TV on and ready to go as soon as the upload went live.

"I'm making it," he said. "Hold your horses."

"It's not my horses I'm worried about. Get in here!"

He was laughing when he carried in the big bowl of popcorn and two glasses of wine. It was a terrible mixture, and she was sure some vintner somewhere would have an absolute fit at the idea of the pairing, but she didn't care right now. Thomas flopped down on the couch next to her and wrapped his arms around her. There was nothing more she could want.

Except for the damn show to start. A year of hard work had seen Jenny Lawson's book brought to life. Olivia had seen a couple of rough cuts, but not the finished work. Evan had offered her an early copy, and she actually had the full first season on a USB drive in her purse, but she wanted to watch the first episode live. With the rest of the world.

As she snuggled into Thomas's arms, the screen lit up with the S&S logo. The next half hour was filled with her dreams. A romantic comedy like she hadn't seen in years. Two people falling for each other. Tension, worries, concern. A cliffhanger ending leading promising that next week's episode would be just as good.

She turned to Thomas with tears in her eyes and found him holding a small velvet box. Her heart started to slam in her chest. "What's..."

"I was going to put it at the bottom of the popcorn bowl or something, but it just seemed too risky," he said. "And I wanted you to know what I was giving you." He popped open the top of the box, and there was that small, sparkling diamond that represented so many of her dreams. What she'd realized over the past year was that the dreams were nothing without him. She'd wanted romance, but she'd never thought all that much about the romantic hero in her life. Now, Thomas was the only person she could imagine having beside her.

He started to shift out from under her, and she grabbed his shirt in both her fists. "I don't you down on one knee," she said. "I want you right here next to me."

"Okay," he said, "okay. I'm not going anywhere."

"But you do have to say it."

He laughed. "Happily. Liv—Olivia, will you make me the happiest man in the world and marry me?"

She practically leapt into his arms, kissing him fiercely, shifting so that she was straddling his lap. "Of course, Thomas," she said. "Yes. Always yes."

He took her left hand and slid the ring into place, then pulled her down for another kiss. She shifted in his lap, grinding just a little, and he made a hungry noise. "Moving around like that is going to give a man ideas."

"Maybe I want to give you ideas," she said. "Maybe the first thing I want to do with your ring on my finger is have you. Right here on this couch."

It wasn't anything new, not really. They'd had sex on basically every surface in the house at this point. When Thomas had moved in, she'd taken a week off work because they couldn't keep their hands off each other. But now, with his ring on her finger, she was going to do it all over again. It would all be new. The weight of that small, sparkling ring on her finger—it didn't change anything, not really, but it changed everything.

"Then you should strip," he said. She did, readily enough. He shrugged out of his clothes and pulled her back into his lap. He was hard, and she was wet enough that he could slip his fingers in her easily, opening her body and making her ready for him. She whimpered as he did, eager and hungry and desperate for him. She moved to pull him into her, but he held her back. "No," he said. "No, beautiful. Not yet."

Those fingers inside her started to move, and he knew how to play her body like a fiddle at this point. He worked her gently, just the way she liked, setting up a rhythm that didn't need to speed up or drive forward, just left her crazed for him. Pleasure was undeniable when he touched her like this. Sometimes he tormented her by slowing down every time he got close, but this time he seemed uninterested in waiting. He drove his fingers into her over and over again, his thumb circling her clit.

"Beautiful," he murmured, using his free hand to lift her breast and catch her nipple between his teeth. "I love it when you crave me."

"Do you?" She gasped, rocking on his hand now. She did every time, trying to make him go faster. He never did.

"I do." He bit down harder, making her shriek. "And do you know what I love more?"

"What?" The pleasure was close now, circling down and pulling her entire body taut. It was hard to move, hard to keep going, but she was a split second away from bursting, she just needed a little bit more, if he would just give her a tiny bit more--

"You still have to work to take my thick cock."

It shattered her, leaving her coming on his hand, gasping and pulsing and slamming herself down on him as she cried out his name. Sparks burst behind her eyes as she tried to catch her breath. She didn't wait, couldn't make herself wait anymore; she shifted herself just enough that his cock pressed against her opening. He pulled her hips forward and was sheathed in her in a heartbeat. He stretched her so painfully and she loved it. Loved that she could take him and loved that it was hard.

"You know," he said, shifting under her, finding a rhythm that would drive them both wild. "I think I'm going to have to have you everywhere in this house. All over again. The bedroom. The shower. The kitchen table."

"Don't forget the office."

"How could I?" He found what he needed, shifted her hips, guiding her so that he was buried deep in her, making her whimper with every thrust. "Your desk. Your chair. The fucking wall. I'm going to have you everywhere, Liv. I'm going to fuck you everywhere in this house. You're mine." He was thrusting fast now, his breath going ragged and harsh. She couldn't keep up with the pace he'd set; she balanced herself on his shoulders as he slammed up into her. Every stroke rubbed at her clit, twisted against that fiery spot inside of her, and she was close again already.

"I'm yours," she whimpered. "I'm going to be yours. I'll always be yours. And you'll be mine." He was grunting with every thrust, wild underneath her. The hand that wasn't steadying her hips was tight on her breast, teasing the nipple, almost hurting but never quite.

"Say it again," he said, his voice tight. "Let me hear you say it."

"I'm yours." The words were sending her in a spiral, high up into the air, her body tightening around him. He groaned, hard, cursing. She could feel him holding back, just barely.

"Again," he said, his teeth clenched.

"I'm yours."

The words sent him over the edge, flooding up into her, and the sensation of him and the way he cursed her name burned through her. He was still gasping and shifting when he found her clit with his thumb, giving her the last little bit she needed to tip over the edge with him, surging around his cock and shattering over him. Collapsing into his arms.

He gathered her up and held her tight. "You're mine," he whispered again, kissing her hair.

"Entirely yours."

A year ago, she'd looked at her life and known that she was satisfied with her career, her company, her work. She'd wanted something more. And now she had it.

The happily ever after of her dreams.

Thank you for reading!

I hope you enjoyed Coffee, Codes, & Cliches

Follow me to stay up to date on what's new.

TikTok: @hannawrites1
Instagram: @authorhannawaldon

Hopeless Series

Book One: Coffee, Codes, & Cliches
Book Two: Coming 2024
Book Three: TBD
Book Four: TBD

Printed in the USA
CPSIA information can be obtained
at www.ICGtesting.com
CBHW021625270724
12235CB00011B/306

9 798868 947193